Permanently
Failing
Organizations

Permanently Failing Organizations

Marshall W. Meyer
Lynne G. Zucker

SAGE PUBLICATIONS
The International Professional Publishers
Newbury Park   London   New Delhi

For information address:

SAGE Publications, Inc.
2111 West Hillcrest Drive
Newbury Park, California 91320

SAGE Publications Ltd.
28 Banner Street
London EC1Y 8QE
England

SAGE Publications India Pvt. Ltd.
M-32 Market
Greater Kailash I
New Delhi 110 048 India

Printed in the United States of America

Library of Congress Cataloging-in-Publication Data

Meyer, Marshall W.
    Permanently Failing organizations / by Marshall W. Meyer and Lynne
  G. Zucker ; foreword by Paul DiMaggio.
        p.   cm.
    Bibliography: p.
    Includes index.
    ISBN 0-8039-3258-8   ISBN 0-8039-3259-6
    1. Organizational behavior.   2. Organizational change.
  I. Zucker, Lynne G.   II. Title.
  HD58.7.M48   1989
  302.3′5—dc19   88-18566
                                                        CIP

SECOND PRINTING 1990

Contents

Foreword

Why do organizations succeed or fail in pursuit of their explicit goals? Few questions bear more pressingly on our collective welfare, and few have been more obdurate to scholarly penetration. Economists and sociologists have defended themselves against acknowledging this obduracy with distinctive mechanisms. Economists as a group employ denial, spinning rational stories about the inevitability of long-run efficiency. Sociologists, for their part, favor flight, skirting the issue rather than facing up to it. In *Permanently Failing Organizations*, Marshall Meyer and Lynne Zucker look performance squarely in the eye and draw on the best of both sociology and economics to explain why some organizations perform well and others perform badly.

The cornerstone of their argument is the union of two familiar observations into an arresting insight. First, organizational mortality declines with age. Second, organizational performance does *not* improve with age. From these two well-established research findings, the authors extract a subversive conclusion: Efficient performance is only one—and not necessarily the most important—determinant of organizational survival. In other words, we are surrounded by organizations whose failure to achieve their proclaimed goals is neither temporary nor aberrant, but chronic and structurally determined.

This conclusion is subversive because, as the authors note, it flies in the face of an assumption that is central to economic theories of industrial competition: that "efficient and effective organizations displace inefficient and ineffective ones." If many organizations perform poorly over long periods of time, an indispensable bulwark of the rational stories upon which many economists rely—the capacity of natural selection to "choose" efficient organizational alternatives—begins to crumble.

Fortunately, this observation is a point of departure, not a conclusion. Rather than content themselves with transdisciplinary nose thumbing, the authors criticize sociologists for avoiding the relationship between selection and efficiency, and emphasizing structural relationships between environments and organizational attributes over studies of process. If natural selection does not favor efficient organizations, why, they ask, is this the case?

The answers to this question occupy most of the volume. Suffice it to say here that organizations attract multiple operative goals—goals that diverge from their official missions and are pursued by employees and external constituencies who wish to use organizations to further their own agendas. When such groups are in a position both to block reorganization and to discourage owners (of proprietary firms), sponsors (of nonprofits), or policy makers (in the public sector) from cashing in their chips, "permanent failure" results. The kind and degree of permanent failure is influenced by an array of factors, including the nature and interests of participating groups, their relationships to one another and capacity for mobilization, the sector in which the organization is located, the clarity of its official mission, and the ease with which performance can be gauged. The story is unavoidably complex, but is clarified and made concrete by reference to four cases that are followed throughout.

The argument is a feat of synthesis, drawing here on population ecology, there on transaction-cost economics or agency theory, elsewhere on resource-dependence or political theories of the firm, bringing into productive confrontation ideas and perspectives that ordinarily run along parallel channels. It is also testimony to the value of intellectual collaboration. The authors are leading figures in their field and their notable previous contributions—Meyer's on bureaucracy and Zucker's on institutional theory—are brought into symbiotic interaction. The book is slender but jammed with arresting insights, questions, and hypotheses about everything from the decline of the steel industry to the latent functions of privatization.

The authors are careful not to claim closure for their account: Their own "official goal," which they accomplish efficiently, is to set out clear and testable hypotheses. The reader is invited to enter into the critical dialogue between the authors as he or she reads. This reader is skeptical of the extent to which U.S. worker's interests are ordinarily reflected in failures of owners to withdraw capital from low-performing firms, given the tenacity of business opposition to even so innocuous a measure as requiring 60 days notice for plant closings. And one wonders if some organizations or agencies do not serve the public interest better by responding to informal member, employee, or constituency claims—that is, by permanently failing—than they would be efficiently pursuing their official missions.

Yet, even if specific points give one pause, the authors have established a framework that clarifies the questions, makes them researchable, and points implicitly to normative as well as positive lines on inquiry. In the proprietary sector, should government regulate, or should the state absorb externalities when welfare considerations make economically "efficient" solutions to firms' problems unpalatable? Under what circumstances can managers of nonprofit organizations or public agencies live with the endemic ambiguity of competing goals; and when must they acknowledge and clarify lines of political and value conflict in order to ascertain and, eventually, to improve performance? Although the authors do not claim to resolve such matters, their work gives us a realistic vocabulary for discussing them.

Permanently Failing Organizations is one of those rare books that speaks at once to the expert, generating fresh insights and fruitful questions from established lines of research, and to the novice, synthesizing literatures and framing crucial problems accessibly and engagingly. It will serve well both to convince students that organizational research is interesting and profoundly relevant to the economic and social challenges of our time, and to establish a theoretical lens and research agenda for scholars willing to confront issues of performance on empirical grounds.

Paul DiMaggio
Yale University

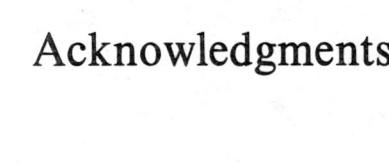

Acknowledgments

Permanently Failing Organizations is the result of several years' collaboration between Marshall Meyer and Lynne Zucker. It reflects continual revision and extension of ideas presented by Meyer to the Department of Management, the Wharton School, University of Pennsylvania and of the initial Meyer-Zucker paper to the American Sociological Association, both in 1985. A revised version of that paper was presented to the Yale University Complex Organizations Workshop in 1986. We wish to thank the participants in these meetings for their helpful comments and criticisms. We are also grateful to Randall Collins, Paul DiMaggio, Jack Hirschleifer, Charles Perrow, and Pamela Tolbert for their extensive written comments on earlier drafts; DiMaggio's comments alone ran 20 single-spaced typewritten pages. We appreciate Hannah Balter's careful artwork on a very rushed schedule. The excellent research assistance of Charles Crary, who conducted the literature search on organizational performance and persistence, is also acknowledged, as is the 1985-1986 UCLA Academic Senate grant to Zucker that funded his work. Finally, we wish to thank Cafe Casino, Westwood, for their policy of unlimited refills, which contributed immeasurably to the ideas developed here.

1. Introduction

This monograph began from two observations. One is commonplace or nearly so: There are many organizations whose performance, by any standard, falls short of the expectations of owners, members, and clients, yet whose existence continues, sometimes indefinitely. Such organizations are often in the public and nonprofit sectors. But they are also found among for-profit firms. The second observation is somewhat more esoteric, drawing from two separate approaches to organizations. One approach is population ecology, a branch of the sociological study of organizations. The other is industrial organization, an established subfield of economics. The observation drawn from these two fields is this: Whereas mortality tends to decline with age for broad classes of organizations—old organizations are *less* likely to die than are young ones—what little evidence there is suggests that performance does not improve correspondingly with age.

These observations are related: There are many low-performing organizations because organizational mortality declines with age while performance does not improve correspondingly. The phenomenon of high-persistence, low-performance organizations has led us to reconsider some ideas that have emerged recently in organizational theory. Of particular concern are concepts of structural inertia (used by economists and sociologists) and institutionalization (used by sociologists). An organization that both persists and performs well is most parsimoniously described as effective. An organization that persists yet performs poorly might be described as inertial or institutionalized, but we prefer to think of such an organization as permanently failing. An organization that persists even though its performance cannot be ascertained may be described as inertial or institutionalized. Ideas about inertia and institutionalization, however, should not obscure the fact that performance constraints exist for almost all organizations, even if these constraints are complicated or inconsistent.[1]

The issue raised in this monograph is whether performance normally takes precedence over other constraints affecting the survival of organizations, or whether performance is subordinated to other constraints. Most theories assume high performing organizations to survive and low performers to fail. But the experience of many organizations suggests otherwise, that low performance is often tolerated because other circumstances prevent owners from closing firms, or public officials from closing obsolete agencies.

The history of the electric interurban railways in the United States is illustrative. These were passenger electric-powered trains that connected cities, mainly operating during the early 1900s. Despite never showing returns over 2 or 3%, generally much lower than alternative investments, the interurban railways were promoted at the turn of the century and again in the 1920s as prime investments. And since they faced similar economic environments, one would expect that the lag between initial unprofitability and closure should be similar for most of the interurbans. In fact, these lag times varied substantially. As Hilton and Due (1964: 243) note, "Theoretically, a company should liquidate when it reaches the stage at which an average return on salvage value exceeds the present and projected return made on the property, and thus before reaching the point of actual losses. . . . Operation for several years at a direct operating loss indicates failure to follow this rule. . . . But clearly many companies operated too long in light of circumstances."

Figure 1.1 presents a graphic record of the lengthy periods some electric interurbans were operated at an operating loss, and the high variance in the number of years of losing operation before abandonment. Contrary to expectations based in economic theory, nearly a third of the interurbans functioned at a loss for five years or more. Clearly, these are permanent failures. For some of these electric interurbans, there are alternative explanations for their continued survival. First, nearly 5% of those showing a loss actually contributed to a co-owned enterprise—such as a real estate venture or lumber mill—that was thriving, creating a side-benefit externality that would keep them in business. Still, there are at least two cases in which the co-owned venture failed, losing money. Others (about 10%) showed very small losses, thus encouraging the owners to hope for a turnaround—though waiting for 10 years or so for a turnaround seems to exceed rational expectations. Thus cases of permanent failures with a "rational" counter explanation account for less than

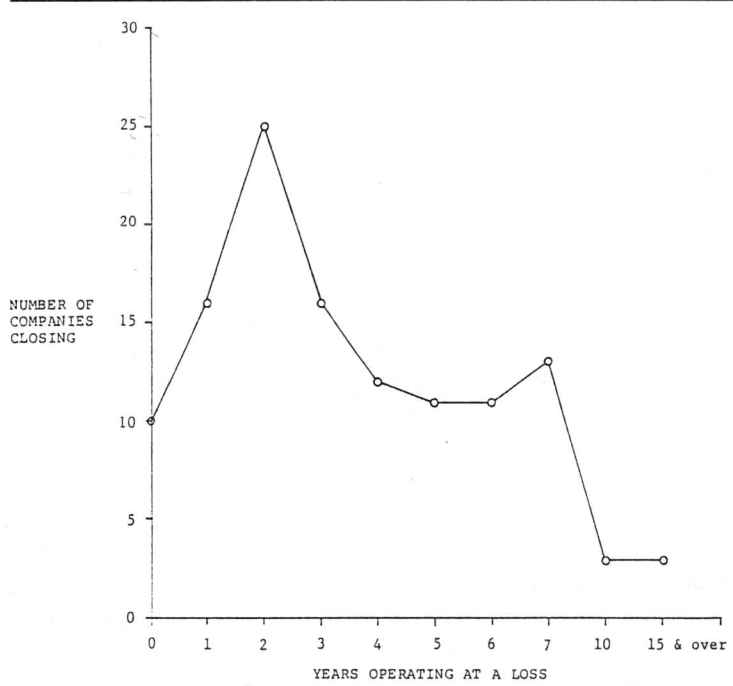

Figure 1.1 Years of Unprofitable Operation Preceding Abandonment for U.S. Electric Interurban Railways, 1906-1958.

15% of the total; at the other extreme are railways, such as the Lake Shore, that had tremendous long-term losses. The Lake Shore accumulated losses of nearly $3 million over an eight-year period. Such losses were made up by exhausting cash reserves and increasing current liabilities through borrowing or deferral of tax payments. As Hilton and Due conclude, "The period of deficit operation for some companies was nothing short of fantastic. The prize must be awarded to the Southern New York, which, after a profit of $16,000 in 1922, operated at a deficit for every one of the 19 years preceding its total abandonment in 1942" (1964: 241).

This monograph cannot answer fully the question of why some nonperforming organizations become permanent failures and others do not, or when performance, in terms of both efficient production and effective garnering of resources, is determinative of organizational persistence and when it is not. A complete answer will require substantial empirical research. But we do suggest how, in general, the combination of high persistence and low performance is possible. We argue as follows: First, diverse interests may arise in and around organizations, particularly when external events cause performance to decline. Second, conflict arising from this division of interests may block organizations from changing established patterns of conduct. Third, sustained low performance results, from which escape is neither easy nor automatic. We also argue that much of the organizational theory and management literatures can be understood as searching for ways to overcome the conditions that drive organizations from initial high performance to sustained low performance. The latter, sustained low performance, is permanent failure.

The idea of permanent failure reverses two key assumptions made conventionally about organizations. One assumption made conventionally is that organizations are, on balance, efficient, or better, that efficient and effective organizations displace inefficient and ineffective ones. Here, we argue that many organizations tend, over time, toward sustained low performance, insofar as performance measures reflect the interests of owners, sponsors (in the case of nonprofit organizations), or the commonweal (in the case of government agencies). We hasten to add that we view permanent failure as a tendency, not an inevitability. Another assumption made conventionally is that organizations act like rational utility-maximizing actors. The metaphor of organizations as rational utility maximizers does not acknowledge that the utilities of the multiple actors in and around organizations are often not the same. But even when diversity of interests is acknowledged, the difficulty of managing diversity is not. Incentives, often unspecified, are assumed capable of aligning otherwise conflicting interests, and, at least for firms, owners are assumed to be sovereign, that is, to control the allocation of incentives. Here, we argue that the participation of multiple actors, whose interests sometimes correspond but sometimes conflict, poses significant problems for the ability of owners (or their equivalents in nonprofit organizations) to impose anything approaching rational utility maximization upon organizations.

Why do organizations become frozen into patterns of low performance? Phrased somewhat differently: Why cannot interests be easily aligned in organizations around performance? The answer, we suggest, is this: Most people are more concerned with maintaining existing organizations than with maximizing organizational performance. As long as performance is high, the interests of those wishing to maintain an organization—often those dependent on it, such as workers or buyers of its product—correspond with those wishing it to meet official objectives (e.g., profit)—often those who control it, such as owners or managers. Indeed, these interests are supportive of one another under conditions of high performance. However, should exogenous events cause performance to deteriorate, which occurs sooner or later in almost all organizations, then the interests of those seeking to maintain organizations and of those seeking high performance become antagonistic, sometimes dramatically so. Those seeking performance—owners vested with property rights or officials having legal authority—attempt to change organizations as external circumstances shift causes and conditions that promote profit-oriented goals. But those wishing to maintain existing organizational arrangements, numerically the majority but not always powerful, oppose change. Change is opposed because of the benefits for the majority, such as good salaries or promotion opportunities. Thus organizations are maintained for reasons of self-interest, not simply inertia, as illustrated by the following example: Suppose owner A employs worker B, and B's productivity has increased over time, and A, accordingly, pays B an above-normal wage. Suppose, further, that B knows his or her skills are unique to A's organization. B therefore has a strong incentive to maintain A in business.[2]

As long as the organization's performance is satisfactory, the interests of A and B correspond. But should performance deteriorate for exogenous reasons, such as supply and demand conditions, and should A wish to liquidate the enterprise, B will use his or her power to maintain the organization in preference to searching for another employer. One question explored in this monograph concerns the circumstances under which B, or better, all B's collectively, can muster sufficient power to maintain the organization despite its low performance.

What is the practical import of the idea of permanently failing organizations? Consider first the problem of productivity, or in its most recent guise, "competitiveness." Our theory of permanent failure does not address causes of innovation and capital investment, which play a substantial role in productivity.[3] The theory does, however, account for why existing technologies and capital are not used to greatest advantage: Workers and other actors associated with organizations often use their power to block changes in the direction of greater productivity, at least when these changes would disrupt their benefits. The theory therefore suggests that some diminution in the power of these dependent actors might yield improved performance, but it also suggests that improved performance may not be an unalloyed good, particularly for those whose private gains require forgoing some changes that might enhance productivity. The theory suggests, finally, that productivity may depend upon two kinds of strategic choices: organizational innovations aimed at limiting the power of dependent actors, and political actions aimed at creating and maintaining an alignment of interests among all of the actors associated with organizations.

Consider second the problem of managing organizations not explicitly focused on pursuing economic efficiency but intended, instead, to pursue other ends, such as advancement of knowledge or of religious doctrine or of public welfare.[4] The theory of permanent failure anticipates why change occurs slowly and with difficulty in these settings. Given diversity on ends or as means to those ends, those wishing change—even when they have formal authority—will often be confronted by others whose interests are served best by nonchange. To the extent that the latter are able to mobilize effectively, stalemate results. The theory also anticipates why many positions, leadership roles in particular, prove so frustrating in these settings. Given the welter of interests represented in organizations whose purpose is not efficiency, all interests are usually served to some degree, but in many cases, no particular interest is served well. All experience sustained low performance on at least some dimensions, though measurement often is difficult and interpretation of these measurements ambiguous. In many of these cases, there will be disagreement as to the cause of permanent failure but not as to its reality.

Perhaps the most important contribution of the theory of permanent failure is the joining of behavioral, largely sociological, and economic perspectives in a way that generates testable hypotheses about the performance of organizations. Behavioral theorists have long been criticized for developing theories about the relation of environmental to structural elements of organizations absent explicit models of optimization or utility maximization. Economists, by contrast, have assumed optimization or utility maximization, largely overlooking structural and political constraints affecting performance. The theory of permanent failure specifies, by contrast, structural and political processes in and around organizations that lead to sustained low performance. It also anticipates that actions such as growth, decentralization, privatization, and renegotiation of employment practices will be taken by owners or managers in order to counter these processes and thereby forestall or reverse low performance. These actions do not occur automatically, however. They require conscious planning, decision making, and implementation. The theory of permanent failure, therefore, unlike most behavioral and economic models of organizations, provides an explicit role for management in organizations.

As in any theoretical endeavor, the ideas developed here are fraught with hazards for research. One difficulty is in the measurement of performance. As noted next, a major problem is whether performance is to be evaluated in terms of official or unstated objectives. We opt for the former, but our choice is somewhat arbitrary.[5] Of even greater difficulty is estimating models in which persistence, normally a dynamic property, is a function of performance, which may be specified either statically or dynamically. (No simple solution to this problem exists—at least yet.) An important function of theory is to draw attention to these hazards and, importantly, the necessity of surmounting them. We expect that some time will be required to develop an empirical basis for the theory of permanent failure. And the theory may prove wrong. But, at a minimum, the theory of permanent failure provides a starting point for thinking and research that joins several formerly separate strands of thinking about organizations, and it provides a theoretical basis for the kinds of management decisions that will inevitably transform the organizational texture of our society.

This monograph is organized as follows. The next chapter presents four cases of permanent failure. Reference is made to these cases throughout the book. In the third chapter, a theoretical basis for permanent failure is established. The chapter begins by examining the assumption of efficiency that pervades much of organizational theory. Diverse rational models assume that organizations seek efficiency because efficient, high-performing organizations survive while others do not. Performance and persistence are asserted to correspond closely and permanently failing organizations are therefore seen to be impossible. The chapter then turns to recent theoretical developments in the sociology of organizations that relax the assumption of efficiency. This recent work is of two sorts. One stream of theorizing, which remains dominant in the sociological perspective, posits environments to pose multiple constraints, rather than a single performance constraint for organizations, and organizations to seek accommodation with these constraints. Another stream of theorizing claims the reverse, arguing that organizations largely create and control their environments, "enacting" them. These developments in the sociology of organizations suggest persistence to be a function of many causes, or, expressed differently, performance to be only one of several sources of organizational persistence.

The fourth chapter reviews research pertinent to the problem of permanent failure. Discussed first are the measurement of organizational performance, which is fraught with complications, and the concomitant of performance identified in research. A parallel section then reviews various measures of persistence and their concomitants. Overall, the causes of persistence and performance appear not to be the same. And some conditions give rise simultaneously to high persistence and low performance. Several exceptional instances, cases in which economists have acknowledged the possibility of high persistence despite low performance, are then reviewed. We argue, however, that a general theory of permanent failure or of organizational maintenance under conditions of low performance is preferable to the ad hoc explanations developed by economists.

The fifth chapter of this monograph develops a theory of permanent failure. The theory explores the maintenance of organizations as a function of divergent interests of owners and dependent actors—the former value performance more and organizational maintenance less than the latter—and the emergence of power among actors normally considered to be dependent upon organizations. Sociological theories of power, collective action, and revolution, which have not previously been applied systematically to issues of organizational persistence and performance, are used to identify conditions under which dependent actors acquire effective power to maintain organizations.

The sixth chapter treats many of the strategic choices made by organizations as well as the doctrine of strategic management itself as responses to the power of dependent actors. This chapter also argues that growth, complexity, and the conflict-ridden character of managerial tasks is best understood within the framework of permanent failure. Organizations are viewed, in sum, as tending toward permanent failure—the combination of high persistence and low performance—owing to the confluence of interests represented in them, while managers are understood as seeking to regain control over or to harmonize these competing interests. The final chapter summarizes the argument and outlines some propositions about the continuing survival of high-persistence, low-performance organizations. We look forward to testing these propositions in research.

Notes

1. Other definitions of performance exist; resource dependency theory, for example, defined effectiveness as survival and capacity to attract resources (Pfeffer and Salancik, 1978). However, we explicitly leave *survival* out of the definition because of obvious confounding of cause and effect, and add the concept of efficiency (input/output maximization). For higher performance, effectiveness and efficiency must covary. In practice, an organization that is very inefficient in production, but that attracts resources, so continues in operation for years, will not be identified as highly performing; nor will an efficient organization that fails after a year because it can't sell its product. Inertial, and some institutionalized organizations, are often inefficient, though they may be very effective as measured by ability to garner resources.

2. B's incentive to maintain A is even greater, and A's performance (at least in terms of profit) is correspondingly weaker to the extent that B has acquired significant learning-by-doing advantages over other possible workers and exploits these advantages to extract even higher wages from A. Note that this does not imply that B wants to maintain *everything* about the organization unchanged, only that B's position is improved when the organization continues to exist and B's "rights" are not infringed upon. In declining industries or economic downturn, when alternatives for B are extremely limited, the value to B of maintaining the organization increases correspondingly.

3. But only to a point: General Motors' investment in automated production technologies appears to have actually *increased* production costs (see *Business Week,* 1987).

4. Some measures of quality in higher education, such as instructional expenditures per student, in fact gauge inefficiency. The more difficult it is to assess official goals, the more difficult it is to select and defend a particular course of action, or any change in it.

5. Performance must be measurable, and it is extremely difficult to determine high performance with multiple or diffuse goals. Thus we place emphasis on the goals of the owners, managers, or others with official responsibility for allocation of organizational resources and/or design of organizational structure.

2. Four Cases of Permanent Failure

In this chapter, four cases illustrating permanent failure are presented. In all four instances, organizations that might reasonably have been discontinued were maintained, if not permanently, at least for a lengthy period of time. The circumstances surrounding permanent failure differ for each of these cases, however. In one case, a metropolitan newspaper remains in business despite declining circulation and advertising revenues. In the second case, an unprofitable meat packing house is sold to its employees and continues to operate—unprofitably—until the employees strike their own company. In a third case, a decision to consolidate three parochial high schools into two because of declining enrollments is thwarted by a coalition of alumni, community groups, and political leaders. In the fourth case, the power of steel firms to shut plants and lay off workers is limited by action on the part of unions, church groups, and the affected communities. The cases are of interest in themselves, but they also serve as concrete illustrations of some abstract principles that will be developed in subsequent chapters.

Case #1: A Declining Newspaper: A Family Divided

The *Los Angeles Herald Examiner* was once the proud flagship of the Hearst publishing empire. There was good reason for pride: The *Herald* was the only newspaper actually founded by William Randolph Hearst (the other Hearst papers, including the *San Francisco Examiner*, were acquired). As recently as 1967, the *Herald's* circulation was nearly 700,000, equal to the *Los Angeles Times*. But the *Herald* was then struck by its unions, and a nine-year struggle followed. Management refused to bargain, and the unions in turn retaliated by urging readers and advertisers to boycott the *Herald*. By the time the strike was settled in 1976, more than half of the readership had been lost—actual circulation was then 300,000 and has since slipped to around 250,000—and advertising lineage had also declined precipitously. The losses in circulation and advertising inevitably rendered the *Herald* unprofitable. Exact figures are not available since the Hearst Corporation is family held, but the *Herald Examiner* is estimated to have lost at least a million dollars a year since the strike and possibly more than 10 million dollars during 1986 alone.

Why are these losses tolerated? One explanation, which cannot be dismissed easily, is the allure of the Los Angeles market. Los Angeles is the second largest city in the United States. "What keeps us there is that it is one of the world's great markets," observed Hearst Corporation's Chairman and CEO, Frank Bennack (*New York Times,* 1987a).[1] But the *Herald's* prospects may be little affected by the growth of Southern California. The *Times* has become the dominant metropolitan daily, and numerous community newspapers (e.g., the *Orange County Register*) have filled the interstices left by the *Times.*[2] The *Herald's* greatest penetration is in south-central Los Angeles, which is predominantly black. Moreover, two-thirds of *Herald* sales are from newspaper racks. The *Herald Examiner* could attempt to recast itself as a newspaper for blue-collar workers along the lines of the *New York Daily News,* but as one former executive noted, "It's hard to do this in a town where the working class speaks Spanish" (personal communcation).

Another explanation for indecision in face of mounting losses is endemic conflict within the Hearst Corporation and family:

> Background interviews with Hearst executives and family members make it clear that the family is divided over the fate of the *Herald*. One faction, led by William Randolph Hearst, Jr. (also known as "Bill"), the 79-year-old editor-in-chief of Hearst Newspapers, is said to be dedicated to the *Herald's* survival but has failed to rally support for a bold attempt to turn the paper around.
>
> Another faction of the Hearst clan is lead by Bill's nephew, George, Jr., a former publisher of the *Herald* who remains bitter over the paper's decline . . . and who is often displeased by the *Herald's* editorial concern for the disadvantaged of society. This group is unable to force sale or closure of the *Herald* but has managed to thwart its efforts to reinvent itself.
>
> Perhaps more decisive than either family faction is the management of the newspaper division under Robert Danzig, which has

not been able to agree on a turnaround formula and lobby it enthusiastically to Bennack, the board and the family [Goodgame, 1987].

Needless to say, conflict and indecision concerning the *Herald Examiner's* fate have sapped staff morale and contributed to high turnover among executives. The *Herald* has had six editors in the last six years, several of whom did not bother to move their families to Los Angeles. At present, the positions of publisher, executive editor, managing editor, and art director remain vacant. Although the Hearst Corporation has generally managed its other properties in a businesslike fashion and has sold some unprofitable newspapers, its treatment of the *Herald* remains remarkably unbusinesslike, much to the detriment of the corporation. As CEO Bennack commented to the *New York Times,* "Though Hearst has done well with its smaller papers, those successes have been dwarfed by the *continuing failure* [our emphasis] of the *Los Angeles Herald Examiner*" (*New York Times*, 1987a).

Case #2: A Bankrupt Meat Packer: Workers Picket Their Own Company

The Rath Packing Company was founded in 1891 and became by the mid-1930s one of the largest meat processors in the United States. In the 1950s, Rath's Waterloo, Iowa plant employed upwards of 7,000 workers and slaughtered 10,000 hogs a day. But the company neglected to invest in new facilities. And, perhaps because of a history of fractious labor relations, Rath was unable to control labor costs in the increasingly competitive market of the 1960s. Rath slipped into unprofitability in the early 1970s and, by 1980, had accumulated losses of $23 million. Partly in response to employee pressures and partly to secure a $4.5 million Federal grant to finance modernization of its plants that was conditioned on employee ownership, Rath's stockholders voted to issue new shares of its stock to its employees, giving them control of the company. A new board was elected, consisting principally of labor representatives, and workers agreed to take $20 per week of their wages in Rath shares (at $2 apiece) rather than cash, a freeze on cost-of-living raises, and termination of their pension plan. By the end of the company's 1980 fiscal year, Rath was able to show a profit, but only because large amounts of wages and benefits had been deferred.

Rath's profitability was short-lived. Even though wages were paid partly in Rath shares, the firm's losses mounted in 1981 and 1982. In early 1983, Lyle Taylor, former president of the United Food and Commercial Workers local representing Rath employees, became president of Rath after employees had agreed to accept a $2.50 per hour wage deferral. But even these steps were insufficient to avert bankruptcy. Rath filed for Chapter 11 protection in early November 1983, after its creditors refused additional loans. Other things being equal, with its creditors at bay and its union agreement, which would have more than restored wages deferred earlier that year, set aside by the bankruptcy court, Rath might have been able to recover. But Rath workers, incensed by changes in work rules at the time their contract was invalidated, began picketing their own company:

> The situation at Rath, which makes an extensive variety of pork and beef products, including bacon, canned and smoked hams and luncheon meats, is far more personal and more bitter than an examination of balance sheets and court actions suggests.
>
> Workers have picketed the plant to protest work rules put into effect when the contract was thrown out by the bankruptcy court judge. Recently, 300 workers struck to protest the dismissal of a worker who refused overtime.
>
> Work goes on at the plant, and the workers often joke and laugh amid the violent, bloody work of slaughter, dismemberment, and processing as the hogs are killed and their carcasses cut into hams, loin roasts and bacon [*New York Times,* 1984a].

But work did not go on at Rath. On December 28, 1984, operations ceased at the Waterloo packing plant. Several proposals for resuscitating Rath were made—one, by management, which would have reorganized the company as a regional packing house with about 500 employees; another, by workers, which would have raised $2 to $4 million from workers to help recapitalize the company. But neither of these plans were acceptable to the bankruptcy court, and Rath went out of business in February 1985.

Even though the Rath Packing Company ultimately failed, it experienced an unusually long period of decline for a firm in a highly competitive industry, almost 15 years. During this period, Rath's operating losses were sustained by borrowing—first from commercial lenders, later from the Federal government, and finally from its own workers. One might ask why workers were willing to sacrifice their wages and pensions to maintain the company.[3] One answer, of course, is that employee ownership had become valued for its own sake, apart from its impact on profitability. Advocates of employee ownership, including Corey Rosen, executive director of the National Center for Employee Ownership, and William Foote Whyte, professor emeritus at the New York State School of Industrial and Labor Relations, claimed that the worker takeover of Rath prolonged its existence. And union officials, in effect, acknowledged this in citing Rath as a case study in the pitfalls of employee ownership: Had traditional patterns of ownership been maintained at Rath, displaced workers would have received severance pay and pension benefits (*New York Times*, 1985).

Case #3: Schools Bereft of Students: Community Sentiment Versus an Archbishop's Business Judgment

Cathedral High School is one of four Catholic secondary schools in central Los Angeles. Owned by the Archdiocese of Los Angeles and operated since 1924 by the Christian Brothers, the teaching order best known for its winery in Northern California, Cathedral High sits just below Dodger Stadium adjacent to the Chinatown district. Cathedral's students have always been immigrant children—initially Italian, now almost entirely Latino. In recent years, 90% of Cathedral's graduates have gone on to college, and many are among the leaders of the Los Angeles Hispanic community. From the standpoint of educational quality, then, Cathedral High was a resounding success; but this was not the primary yardstick used by the achdiocese to measure its performance, as we shall see.

Until recently, Cathedral High has not had difficulty filling its places. But the other three diocesan boys' schools in central Los Angeles suffered significant enrollment declines in the early 1980s, and consolidations or mergers appeared to be inevitable. Even so, when it was revealed in early July 1984 that the archdiocese had entered into a contract to sell Cathedral High School to a Hong Kong developer—without consulting the Christian Brothers—the school's students, staff, and alumni were shocked, galvanizing a successful "Save Cathedral High" campaign.

The decision to close Cathedral High School was consistent with the businesslike approach to most matters taken by the Los Angeles Archdiocese. Monsignor Benjamin Hawkes, vicar general of the archdiocese, had built the archdiocese into the second wealthiest in the United States through several decades of development, building, and real estate transactions. Cathedral High occupies one of the most valuable plots in Los Angeles. The agreed sale price for the seven-acre property was not revealed, but was estimated at about $10 million, many times the value of the other diocesan schools in central Los Angeles. Moreover, Cathedral was the oldest of the campuses and required extensive renovations to bring its structures into conformity with Los Angeles's earthquake codes.

What made business sense to the archdiocese was anathema to Cathedral's supporters, who took their case first to the Los Angeles City Council. Less than two weeks after news of the planned sale surfaced, Cathedral's supporters obtained a council vote directing the planning department and the Community Redevelopment Agency to prepare zoning studies that delayed development of the school property for at least a year. And 10 days later, in early August 1984, the council declared Cathedral High School a cultural monument, preventing demolition of the buildings for an even longer period. These actions were shortly followed by a superior court suit alleging that the land occupied by the school had been unlawfully transferred from the city to the archdiocese in the nineteenth century and therefore could not be sold.

The fate of Cathedral High remained uncertain for almost 18 months. In December 1985, the archdiocese announced that it had reconsidered its decision to sell the property. The *Los Angeles Times* reported as follows:

> Archbishop Roger Mahoney, ending a controversy that had deeply disturbed many Latino Catholics here for more than a year, announced Tuesday that he has decided not to close Cathedral High School, the alma mater of generations of successful immigrants' sons.
>
> Mahoney's decision reverses the position of his predecessor, Cardinal Timothy Manning, who retired in September. Manning had quietly agreed to sell the preparatory school to a Hong Kong developer for $10 million and had denied impassioned pleas by alumni and community members to save the 62-year-old all-boys school, which had been scheduled to close in 1987.
>
> Tuesday's announcement marked a dramatic finale to 18 months of public controversy that began last year when news of the sale leaked out to Cathedral students and alumni.
>
> Thousands of people, mainly Latinos, contributed $30,000 in small donations for a "Save Cathedral High" campaign. Friends of Cathedral, spearheading the effort, took out newspaper ads, rented dozens of billboards, and organized demonstrations. Students and family members arranged for special Masses [*Los Angeles Times*, 1985].

Not reported by the *Times* or any other newspaper is the archdiocese's reluctance to close any school in order to consolidate operations in the aftermath of the Cathedral High episode. At the present time, Cathedral is operating at 85% of capacity, with 413 students, while the other three diocesan high schools in central Los Angeles are at well below 50% capacity, leaving more than a thousand empty seats. An official of the archdiocese has stated flatly that there is no possibility that Cathedral High School will be sold. The same official has also indicated that the archdiocese "will not initiate discussion of closing any schools," and that any proposals for mergers or consolidations will have to come from the schools themselves. Underenrolled schools, therefore, have become a fact of life for the Los Angeles Archdiocese, though we suspect that the final chapter in consolidation has not yet been written.

Case #4: The Natural History of a Declining Industry: Ownership Prerogatives Redefined

Increased foreign competition coupled with the aging of U.S. steel plants have produced a situation in which most U.S. steel manufacturers were no longer competitive in world markets in the late 1970s. Steel plants yielded at best a much lower rate of return than alternative investments by the mid-1980s. If fact, most of the larger steel companies were showing negative returns, illustrated by U.S. Steel's (USX) operating loss of $1.37 billion from its steel operations in 1986 (*New York Times,* 1987b).

Steel companies responded to continuing losses by laying off workers and closing plants. From 1979 to 1984, employment in the steel industry dropped 52% (American Iron and Steel Institute, *Annual Statistical Report, 1985*: 30-31). U.S. Steel reported white collar staff reductions of about 60% from 1982 to 1986. And during this period, many more workers were placed on permanent layoffs, a device used to delay pension and other termination expenses. Membership in the United Steel Workers also dropped by half in this period (*New York Times,* 1986a).

The declining fortunes of the U.S. steel industry would have resulted in even more plant closings and layoffs but for resistance of unions, employees, and affected communities. This resistance ultimately took the form of creating quasi-governmental bodies, such as Pennsylvania's Steel Valley Authority. These agencies acted aggressively to limit the rights of steel and other companies to dispose of plants and workers no longer producing profits for them. Union and worker sacrifices in wages have been replaced by profit sharing and stock ownership plans, partnership relations with management, and, in some cases, board memberships (*New York Times,* 1986a, 1986b).

While a brief summary cannot begin to do justice to the tumultuous history of the "steel revolt" of the 1980s, it can convey some of the flavor of events. Late in the 1970s, new organizations were created to oppose the shutdown process, including the Tri-State (Pennsylvania, Ohio, and West Virginia) Conference on Steel, which grew out of the Ecumenical Coalition formed in response to closures in Ohio. The steelworkers who formed the nucleus of this group organized a campaign against corporate decisions to close plants and encouraged public ownership of plants that could not be operated profitably, perhaps modeled after Conrail's takeover of the Eastern rail lines.

Three principal strategies were adopted by organizations opposed to steel plant shutdowns. One strategy advocated boycotts of firms believed inimical to workers' interests. Boycotts were supported by an aggressive campaign led by ministers, including Reverend John J. Gropp, whose dismissal by his bishop caused militant steelworkers to blockade his church in order to prevent Gropp's removal by the sheriff. This ministry group, whose principal targets were U.S. Steel and the Mellon Bank, continued to defy church leaders even after some of its key members were jailed (*New York Times,* 1983, 1984b, 1984c, 1984d).

A second major strategy was to encourage the firms to reconsider their decisions, and to find ways to keep even marginally profitable plants open. The Tri-State Conference on Steel targeted the U.S. Steel decision to demolish the huge blast furnace (Dorothy Six) at Duquesne, Pennsylvania. They succeeded in having studies of the feasibility of reactivating the blast furnace commissioned by both the Steelworkers and U.S. Steel. Although these studies concluded independently that it would not be economical to reactivate this facility, statements from key managerial personnel of U.S. Steel made it clear that the company was now more receptive to maintaining marginally profitable plants.[4] Concern with community relations and potentially negative publicity caused this shift in attitudes.

A third strategy was to facilitate public ownership or, better, to threaten seizure of the steel mills by public bodies. Working with the Tri-State Conference, the Pittsburgh City Council had earlier moved to take the property of Nabisco by eminent domain. Nabisco announced its intent to close its Pittsburgh plant in late 1982. Within a week of Mayor Caliguiri's announcement of support for the eminent-domain action, motivated by concern for both workers and the city's tax base, Nabisco reversed its decision to close the plant.

But the eminent-domain strategy was not to remain confined to local government. The Steel Valley Authority, chartered by the Commonwealth of Pennsylvania, was incorporated in February 1986 with authority to issue bonds and exercise powers of eminent domain (*New York Times,* 1986c). The formation of the Steel Valley Authority stimulated companies to develop alternatives to closure, including selling three smaller plants no longer wanted by U.S. Steel to a new independent producer (*New York Times*, 1986). The Steel Valley Authority also used court injunctions to block closure of the Union Switch and Signal and WABCO plants, backed by local communities who viewed these shutdowns as "bombshells."

Conflict and sustained low performance.   What, one might ask, do these cases have in common? After all, one concerns a family business, one a business in which employees assumed ownership, the third a school in which business considerations are, at least in principle, secondary to other purposes, and the fourth several large firms in a declining industry. An element common to these cases is, of course, sustained low performance, the maintenance of organizations that in one way or another fell short, sometimes dramatically so, of official objectives. The *Herald Examiner,* Rath Packing, and the steel industry were losing money rapidly. And while Cathedral High had been quite successful through the early 1980s, its decline was nearly as inevitable as the decline in the larger system of Catholic (as well as in public) education. Another common element is divergence between *stated* objectives and the interests of those in some way dependent on the organization, whether for prestige, wages, or church-based education. In all four cases, these divergences became most salient when decisions about how to reorganize or shut these organizations approached. In the case of the *Herald,* the status of the Hearst family was in some sense tied to its continuation, causing disagreements within the family. Rath experienced conflict among its worker-owners as conditions deteriorated. The proposed sale of Cathedral High School triggered a debate that involved much of the Hispanic community and the political leadership of Los Angeles. And political conflict of even greater intensity, as evidenced by the formation of several political action organizations, surrounded the actual and proposed closures of major steel facilities in the Pittsburgh area.

In the next chapters, we shall explore the relationship of divergent interests to permanent failure. At this point, we need only suggest that the link between the two is not as simple as it might seem, that while low performance often causes latent differences in interests among constituencies associated with organizations to become manifest, these differences, once manifest, often have the unplanned and unanticipated effect of sustaining low-performing organizations.

Notes

1. While this statement indicates the Hearst Corporation's desire to stay in the Los Angeles market, one would be hard pressed to argue that this is a primary or even secondary objective of this organization.

2. This case illustrates rather nicely Glenn Carroll's arguments concerning resource partitioning (Carroll, 1984b).

3. The lack of alternative jobs in the local community is one obvious reason.

4. See Harvard Business School cases on the United States Steel Corporation and the Steel Valley Authority: #9-386-171 and #9-386-172, 6/86. HBS Case Services, Harvard Business School, Boston, MA 02163.

3. Performance and Persistence
in Organizational Theory

The title of this monograph—*Permanently Failing Organizations*—is deliberately provocative. It is also a contradiction. How can organizations be at once utterly permanent yet utter failures? Obviously they cannot be. But short of total failure are numerous organizations that are also chronic low performers, that chronically fail to meet official objectives such as showing a profit or providing efficient public service, yet somehow persist for a long time, sometimes forever. Organizations of this sort are the subject of this monograph.

Permanently failing organizations abound. Examples include schools and colleges that never fill their classrooms, bureaucracies having no palpable functions, and unprofitable firms, some requiring government subsidies in order to stay afloat.[1] Organizations are not permanent failures simply as a result of temporary lapses from efficient and effective conduct (Hirschman, 1970) that often occur in periods of recession or technological change. Permanent failure sets in when there is little expectation that efficient and effective conduct will be restored (or, to use different language, that recuperation will take place), yet there is little serious disruption of existing organizational patterns.[2] John Due's (1977: 28) description of U.S. short-line railroads is instructive: "The owners of many short line roads have continued to operate them far beyond the time at which strictly economic conditions would dictate abandonment."

What sustains permanently failing organizations, organizations that are at best marginally profitable or marginally successful in meeting other objectives? Permanently failing organizations, we argue, yield benefits that motivate investment in and maintenance of them, but these benefits often accrue to those who are in one way or another dependent on organizations rather than to those who legally own or control them. In cases in which dependent actors' motivation to preserve low-performing organizations is transformed into effective power to do so, permanent failure results.

Our interest in permanently failing organizations, units characterized by high persistence yet low performance, stems from cases in which "who benefits" comes into question, as well as from organizational theory and research. Consider the following:

- Theory is divided between rational and nonrational models of organizational behavior, the former assuming performance determinative of persistence, the latter ignoring performance, thereby assuming it irrelevant. Theory has not addressed explicitly whether there is a middle ground, whether for some organizations under some conditions performance is only one of many constraints and does not necessarily determine survival. One way to explore this middle ground, we shall argue, is to begin thinking of performance and persistence as separable and possibly independent properties of organizations.

- Research has been divided between studies measuring performance directly or assuming performance constraints, and studies focusing on persistence but taking little or no account of performance. It is important to note that few research studies have examined the relationship of performance to persistence, and those that have done so have yielded results that are mixed at best; most indicate that performance declines with increasing organization and age. In this monograph, we shall argue that the results from recent studies of persistence, in conjunction with evidence from research on performance, show persistence and performance sometimes having different causes and therefore differing and in some instances diverging dramatically from one another.

- Finally, we believe that the phenomenon of permanently failing organizations illuminates some fundamental dynamics of organizations: First, the motivation to maintain organizations may be much greater among actors normally considered to be dependent upon organizations, especially under conditions of low performance, than among owners or residual claimants valuing only performance; second, this motivation may, under some circumstances, be transformed into effective power, rendering poor performance insufficient to dislodge organizations; and, third, many of the strategic choices made by organizations are aimed at offsetting the power of dependent actors and thus relieving permanent failure. These dynamics, we believe, account not only for the weak relationship of performance to persistence observed empirically, but also for the greater mortality rates of small compared to large organizations, and the tendencies of firms to adopt the multiunit and conglomerate forms of organization and of governments to privatize delivery of certain services despite inconsistent evidence concerning efficiency gains from such changes.

Our fundamental hypothesis differs dramatically from much conventional thinking about organizations. Reduced to its essentials, the conventional view in both the sociological and economic literatures contains two assertions. The first is that organizations strive to elicit maximally efficient conduct from their members. For sociologists this is the control problem, for economists the agency problem: How does one plan, supervise, and reward the work of nonowners so that they act in the interest of owners (or, in economists' language, residual claimants)? The second assertion is that organizations eliciting maximally efficient conduct survive whereas others do not. This is an affirmation of faith, which is implicit in the sociological literature and explicit in economics (and which, needless to say, we are about to challenge). Neither of these assertions is considered problematic, yet together they render permanent failure impossible.

The hypothesis proposed here, by contrast, is that maximally efficient conduct is often not attained and sometimes not even sought for the simple reason that organizations are valued and preserved to the extent that they provide benefits to owners *and* nonowners, assuming the two can be distinguished.[3] Since some benefits (especially profit) are synonymous with performance, others (growth, prestige, employment) may be unrelated to financial performance, and still others (slack, accrued pension benefits, "rents" of office or above-normal wages, below-normal prices) clearly detract from performance at least in firms, the relationship of overall organizational performance to organizational persistence is cloudy at best, and in some instances may be inverse. Permanently failing organizations characterized by high persistence yet low performance are thus possible.

The possibility of permanent failure—high persistence yet low performance—precludes equating performance with survival or, for that matter, reproductive success.[4] Defining what performance is, as will be shown next, poses much greater difficulty than defining what it is not. Clearly, however, organizational performance is a function of attainment of objectives or goals—which raises the question of whose objectives, whose goals are the benchmarks against which performance is assessed. For the most part, and consistent with the bulk of the organizational literature, we assume official objectives or goals, such as profit or public service, in the following discussion. But unofficial objectives, particularly the maintenance of existing organizational patterns, are central to our theory of permanent failure.

Our analysis of the relationship of organizational performance to persistence begins with a sketch of two broad classes of theorizing. One assumes efficiency in organizations. The other treats efficiency as one of several possible outcomes of interactions between environments and organizations.

The Assumption of Efficiency

The assumption of efficiency pervades much of organizational theory. This assumption contains at least two hypotheses. One hypothesis is that organizations, in fact, seek efficiency. A second hypothesis is that organizations failing to attain efficiency are somehow jeopardized. What sort of jeopardy faces inefficient organizations is not specified. At the extreme is total collapse, but other possibilities can be imagined. We shall explore these two hypotheses separately.

Organizations seek efficiency.   The notion that organizations seek efficiency pervades both the sociological and economic literatures on organizations, albeit with somewhat greater specificity in the latter. The traditional sociological perspective, stemming from Weber's (1946) work on bureaucracy, takes the existence of organizations as evidence of their superior efficiency compared to other means of coordinating human conduct.[5] Moreover, once in existence, this perspective views incremental adjustments within individual organizations as preserving and perhaps augmenting their efficiency advantages. That organizations have efficiency advantages has not been accepted uncritically by all sociologists. Some, in fact, argue that organizations are in practice often dysfunctional (Merton, 1940; Crozier, 1964). However, preservation, if not optimization, of efficiency advantages has been assumed in empirical studies of organizational structures and of organization-environment relations.[6] To be sure, sociologists have been aware that some organizations have goals, such as effective treatment, that do not encompass efficiency (Blau and Scott, 1962; Etzioni, 1975) and that people in organizations often pursue objectives other than efficiency,[7] but the core of organizational theory and tests of this theory have, until recently, preserved the notion that efficiency takes precedence over other outcomes.

The stance of economics toward organizations—of any kind—has been marked with ambivalence. To be sure, the primacy of efficiency or utility considerations has been maintained throughout. But efficiency or utility maximization has been assumed more characteristic of individual persons than of organizations. Neoclassical economic thinking has for the most part assumed away the problem of the firm. More extreme, the Austrian school of economics and its followers have treated bureaucratic administration as inefficient compared to market coordination of activity, much in contrast to Weber's claims for the superior efficiency of bureaucracy (von Mises, 1944; Downs, 1967; Niskanen, 1971; 1975).

Recently and largely in response to the growth of large business enterprises, the positive contributions of administrative organization to efficiency have been emphasized by economists. No single model has been able to explain definitively the efficiency advantages of organizations over nonorganizational modes of coordination. There are rather a variety of theories. Three are of particular interest here, including shirking-control, transactional, and agency models of organizations. They will be described seriatim.

- Organizations as devices to control shirking (see Alchian and Demsetz, 1972). The theory of organizations as devices for controlling shirking—the deliberate withholding of effort—addresses the question of why supervision and management are necessary at all. The theory maintains the neoclassical assumption of utility maximization at the individual level, but it assumes two further conditions: first, that people must be organized into teams in order to achieve the greatest efficiencies, and, second, that team production is fraught with nonseparabilities whereby the outputs of individual members are not easily gauged. When individual outputs cannot be ascertained, there is strong temptation to allow others to carry the burden of work. The remedy for shirking is monitoring or metering or direct supervision of work. Since supervisors as well as workers may be prone to shirking, monitoring or metering of their activities may also be necessary. Organizational hierarchies therefore arise.

- Organizations as transactionally efficient (see Williamson, 1975; 1981; 1985). The transactional model attempts to explain both why organizations arise in the first place and why they assume different forms. The transactional perspective amends neoclassical theory even more severely than does the theory of organizations as shirking-control devices, for it insists that economic exchanges themselves, not only the goods and services exchanged, are costly. Least-cost forms of exchange are therefore sought. Market exchanges often minimize transaction costs but do not always do so; sometimes market imperfections compel exchanges within organizations. Moreover, depending upon circumstances, some organizational forms may offer greater transactional efficiencies than others, depending upon circumstances. The fundamental proposition of transaction cost theory states that organizations arise when markets fail; conversely, extant organizational forms that are transactionally inefficient may be displaced by markets or, alternatively, new organizational forms. The intersection of specific individual and environmental elements determines transaction costs, hence the relative efficiency of markets and alternative organizational forms.

- Organizations as agents of ownership interests (see Jensen and Meckling, 1976; Fama, 1980; Fama and Jensen, 1983a; 1983b). Agency theories of organizations attempt to explain the separation of ownership from day-to-day control that is characteristic of many business firms, and thereby amend the neoclassical assumption that organizations function like single entrepreneurs. Like transaction-cost theory, agency theory begins from the premise that contracts are not costlessly written and enforced. But unlike the transactional approach, an organization is viewed as a collection or "nexus" of contracts rather than an alternative to contracting. At issue in agency theory is the connection between internal decision making and the participation of "residual claimants" to whom profits (or losses) flow and in whose interest the organization operates. The basic hypothesis is this: When risk-bearing "residual claimants" are not involved in day-to-day decision making, decision making tends to be separated from ultimate control of decisions. Conversely, when the same persons both make and exercise ultimate control over decisions, then these persons tend also to be the "residual claimants." Separation of decision making from ultimate decision control occurs under conditions of complexity for many conventional reasons, such as specialization of knowledge but also minimization of risk: Consistent with financial portfolio theory, "residual claimants" rationally spread their investments across several organizations, limiting their participation in routine decision making.

These three economic theories differ substantially with respect to what they seek to explain (supervision, organizational hierarchy, separation of ownership from control) as well as to the specific causes giving rise to these features of organizations (shirking, transaction costs, risk reduction). They share, however, the assumption that efficient outcomes are preferred to inefficient outcomes. Thus for example, efficiency considerations give rise to supervision in which shirking occurs, to hierarchy in which market transactions prove inefficient, and to passive ownership in which specialization and complexity pose risks requiring that assets be distributed across several firms. Nowadays, if not previously, organizations are understood by economists as promoting rather than impeding efficiency outcomes.[8]

Efficient organizations survive.   The hypothesis that efficient organizations survive complements the hypothesis that organizations, in fact, seek efficiency. It is maintained by both sociologists and economists. Penrose (1952: 810), summarizing Alchian (1950), writes: "Positive profits can be treated as the criterion of natural selection—the firms that make profits are selected or 'adopted' by the environment, and others are rejected and disappear." Thompson (1967: 1) notes, "Organizations do some of the basic things they do because they must—or else!" Williamson states repeatedly that the efficiency properties of alternative organizational forms (including nonorganizational or market transactions) determine their success or failure. Fama and Jensen (1983b: 327) are even more direct: "Absent fiat, the form of organization that survives in an activity is the one that delivers the product demanded by customers at the lowest price while covering costs."

The linkages between organizational efficiency and survival, unlike linkages between organizational form and efficiency, are poorly specified in theory save for the most general observations: Efficient producers—that is, firms producing goods at least cost— drive out high-cost producers due to two causes. First, markets favor low prices. High-cost producers, whose costs are reflected in perfect competition, in shrunk profits will be bereft of cash; in imperfect competition, high-cost producers who increase prices will be bereft of customers. Second, firms cannot withstand losses of profits or of customers, at least not for long.[9]

The assumption that only efficient organizations survive raises several questions. One concerns the definition of failure. Broadly, two types of failures can be conceived, those that do not disrupt the ordinary operations of an organization and those that do. Among the former are internal reorganization, change of ownership, and reorganization of debt under bankruptcy statutes. The more disruptive forms of failure include partial or total liquidation of assets, and cessation of operations. Clearly, most organizations (although not necessarily creditors) will prefer the less to the more disruptive forms of failure. But whether the former constitute failure in the sense intended in theory is open to debate. We consider the less disruptive forms explicitly to constitute survival, since benefits to dependents generally flow uninterrupted, although not necessarily unmodified.

Another question concerns whether the two sources of failure associated with inefficiency operate with equal force. A reasonable hypothesis is that firms can withstand temporary financial losses better than they can withstand permanently lost customers. A third question concerns how long an interval of inefficiency precedes failure. The connection between inefficiency and failure is closest in perfectly taut markets, which permit no time for lapsed organizations to recuperate. Since recuperation does occur in some instances, the connection between inefficiency and failure is less than instantaneous.[10]

The relationship of performance to persistence.   The assumption of efficiency, which pervades much of the organizational literature but particularly the work of economists, yields an expected relationship of performance to persistence. High-performing organizations will survive, whereas low performers will not. Figure 3.1 depicts this expected relationship. As can be seen in the Figure 3.1, virtually all organizations fall on the major diagonal—the low persistence-low performance and high-persistence high performance cells.

A More Differentiated View of Organizations and Their Environments

We now turn to models that relax somewhat the insistence that organizations seek only efficiency outcomes. Because multiple constraints replace the single imperative of efficiency maximization in these models, the constraints posed by environments are specified explicitly. In place of organizations pursuing the undifferentiated objective of efficiency in environments that are likewise undifferentiated (and therefore unspecified), variation in objectives both within and across organizations in response to diverse external influences is posited. The maintained hypothesis is that organizations managing environmental constraints most successfully are also best able to attain their objectives. In most cases, effective management of external constraints is assumed to occur through organizational

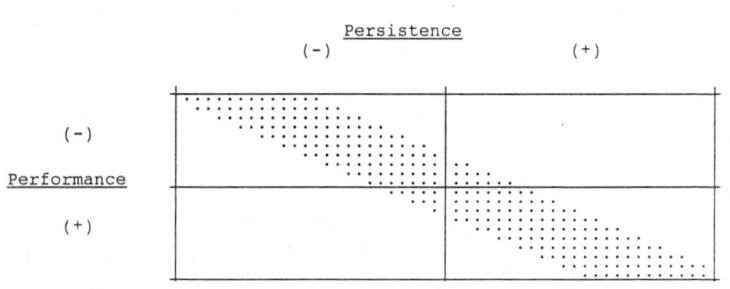

Figure 3.1   The Relationship of Performance to Persistence Under the Assumption of Efficiency

isomorphism with environments, but some models treat organizations as agents capable of constructing and controlling their own environments rather than the reverse.

Organizational isomorphism with environments.   The assumption of isomorphism substitutes for efficiency imperatives the notion that organizations must fit or correspond in critical respects to their environments in order to maintain resource flows. Three arguments asserting organization-environment isomorphism are theories of performance, of survival, and of organizational legitimation.

• Performance as contingent upon organization-environment isomorphism. Early theories asserting environmental determination of organizations assumed an efficiency imperative, but in a much weaker form than that assumed in the efficiency models reviewed here: Efficiency outcomes are dependent upon certain specific correspondences between organizational and environmental elements generally overlooked in economic models. Contingency models, in particular, argued that the fit of organization to technologies and to environmental elements should be strongly associated with performance. Thus it was argued that highly differentiated and volatile environments demand highly differentiated and therefore highly coordinated organizations for effective performance (Lawrence and Lorsch, 1967), and that high levels of technological advancement also demand relatively elaborate organizational structures to maximize performance (Woodward, 1965). A causal chain from environment to organization to efficiency outcomes was thus hypothesized, somewhat more elaborate than the efficiency models of economists.

- Survival as contingent upon organization-environment isomorphism. Another set of theories treats organizations as seeking isomorphism with environments in order to maximize survival chances. Performance or efficiency outcomes are not wholly disregarded, but are subordinated to survival on two grounds, one logical, one substantive. The logical argument is straightforward: The existence of individual organizations or of populations of organizations precedes their performance characteristics. The substantive argument may be of greater interest: Given variation or uncertainty in environments, organizations sometimes engage in inefficient conduct, such as accumulating slack resources, in order to ride out later intervals of uncertainty. Following Hannan and Freeman (1977), organizational forms can be classified crudely as specialists or generalists. Specialists engage in limited activities, do not accumulate slack or idle capacity, and perform efficiently. Generalists, by contrast, engage in multiple activities, accumulate slack and idle capacity, and tend therefore, at any point in time, to perform less efficiently than specialists. But Hannan and Freeman develop specific hypotheses suggesting that under some conditions, generalists, despite lower efficiency on average, will be favored over specialists in rates of survival.[11]

- Legitimation as contingent upon organization-environment isomorphism. A third set of theories of organizational isomorphism removes efficiency even further from consideration. Whereas earlier theories treated first efficiency and later survival as outcomes of correspondences between organizations and their environments, recent thinking has focused instead on the ways in which the appearance of reasonableness and rationality is sustained. Implicitly, the possibility of truly rational conduct is denied, because "rationality" is socially constructed. The external referent of organizational action consists not of tangible elements in the environment but of ideas about how large-scale activities ought rationally to be conducted. A number of specific propositions flow from the hypothesis that organizations strive to maintain legitimacy by conforming to institutionalized beliefs about how they ought rationally to be constructed.[12] For example, schools must hire certified, properly credentialed teachers, or they will be disaccredited, causing dramatic loss of resources.

A somewhat different version of this theory treats organizations as seeking isomorphism with other organizations rather than with institutionalized beliefs as to how they ought rationally to be constructed. "Mimetic processes" posited by DiMaggio and Powell (1983) are said to render organizations legitimate to the extent that they resemble others in the same sphere or sector of activity.[13] Interestingly, and for reasons to be discussed next, it has also been argued that imitation of other organizations may also contribute directly to survival rather than contributing only indirectly through legitimation.

The impact of organizations on environments.   Some theories have relaxed the assumption that environments determine organizations, either by treating organizations as having relatively high power over their relevant environments or by treating environments as poorly organized or irrelevant. In the first case, the extent of an organization's continuing control over its own boundaries is assumed to determine the amount of environmental penetration. Firms use boundary units, contracting, and other means to reduce their vulnerability to external forces (Thompson, 1967: chap. 3; Thompson and McEwen, 1958). Government agencies often make use of cooptation (Selznick, 1949).

In the second case, environmental constraints are assumed to be relatively weak. This is articulated in different ways: (1) control by the surrounding environment is not as legitimate as control by the organization itself (Clark, 1983); (2) organizational systems are in fact self-contained and have few real dependencies on the environment (Luhmann, 1982, 1985, on self-referencing systems); (3) organizations define structure in response to perceived problems, not environmental imperatives (Meyer et al., 1985, on the "problem-organization-problem-more organization" cycle of bureaucratic growth); (4) organizations are extremely powerful collective actors, sometimes controlling the environment and sometimes even dominating it (Coleman, 1974; Dowling and Pfeffer, 1975).

The relationship of performance to persistence.   The more differentiated view of organizations and their environments yields a somewhat weaker relationship of performance to persistence than is expected under the assumption of efficiency. This relationship is depicted in Figure 3.2. The assumption of isomorphism between organizations and environments anticipates efficiency, survival, and legitimacy outcomes, but these different outcomes are not necessarily connected to one another. Indeed, actions taken to promote efficiency (e.g., a specialist strategy) may be antithetical to survival in some instances. And some models remove environmental constraints altogether from organizations themselves, rendering the expected relationship of performance to persistence uncertain at best.

Summary of Theoretical Perspectives

Table 3.1 summarizes the efficiency and more differentiated models of organizations reviewed here. The maintained hypothesis in efficiency models is that efficient units survive. Derivative hypotheses identify organizational mechanisms contributing to efficiency. The maintained hypothesis in most of the more differentiated models of organizations is that environments constrain organizations. Derivative hypotheses identify outcomes of organization-environment isomorphism, including efficiency, survival, and legitimation. An alternative hypothesis is that organizations exercise power over environments. As one moves in Table 3.1 from the efficiency to more differentiated models of organizations, the connection of performance to organizational persistence weakens, indeed disappears at some point. The combination of high persistence with low performance, permanently failing organizations, increases in likelihood as one moves from the top toward the bottom of Table 3.1. Theoretical

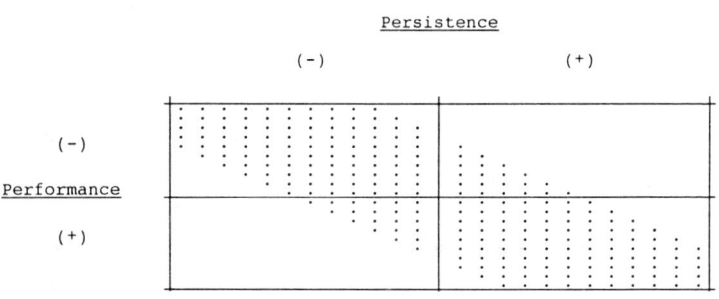

Figure 3.2   The Relationship of Performance to Persistence Under More Differentiated Models

TABLE 3.1

Efficiency and Nonefficiency Models of Organizations

Efficiency Models

Maintained hypothesis:
   organization → efficiency → survival
Derived hypotheses:
   (a) shirking control → organization → efficiency → survival
   (b) transaction costs → organization → efficiency → survival
   (c) risk-bearing → organization → efficiency → survival

More Differentiated Models

(1) Maintained hypothesis (assuming organizational isomorphism with environments):
   environment → organization
Derived hypotheses:
   (a) environment → organization → efficiency
   (b) environment → organization → survival
   (c) environment → organization → legitimation

(2) Maintained hypothesis (assuming organizational power over environments):
   organization → environment

analysis alone, of course, cannot ascertain whether there are large numbers of permanently failing organizations and under what circumstances they appear. For this reason, we turn now to research on organizational performance and persistence.

Notes

1. The Italian government publishes from time to time a list of useless bureaucracies, among them an agency charged with administering pensions for the widows of the Garibaldi wars (which ended in the early 1860s).

2. Changes in ownership sometimes occur in response to low performance, as in employee buyouts or the transfer of assets to new owners. Changes affecting control, such as increased worker participation in employee owned firms (Hochner and Granrose, 1985), may also take place. For present purposes, these kinds of changes will be understood as not seriously disrupting organizational patterns, hence not affecting the existence of an organization. While some shift in goals may occur, such as worker owned firms stressing job preservation, bank loan officers are unlikely to accept these as "reasonable" goals, and are unwilling to provide capital on that basis.

3. Exit may be a cheap strategy: Owners may reinvest capital, workers can find other jobs. But when costs are higher, or equivalent jobs scarce, motivation to maintain the organization increases.

4. In the domain of human sociobiology, the criterion of reproductive success has been shown to yield absurd inferences (Winter 1986).

5. It should be noted that Weber's account of bureaucracy is in this respect inconsistent with his ideal-typical method; whereas Weber could have argued merely that ideally, that is, ideationally, bureaucracy embodies the value of efficiency in administration, he chose to make the empirical claim that bureaucracies are in fact more efficient than are alternatives.

6. See, on this point, Woodward (1965), Lawrence and Lorsch (1967), and Blau and Schoneherr (1971). In each case, observed relations among elements of organizational structure or between these elements and environmental elements are assumed to promote efficient operations.

7. Numerous studies of so-called informal organization (e.g., Roethlisberger and Dickson, 1939) testify to this last point.

8. One irony should not go unnoticed, namely that contemporary economics and classical—but not contemporary—sociology converge

on this point. See Meyer (1987) for a discussion of how economists and sociologists have reversed their respective positions on the efficiency of organizational hierarchies.

9. The latter may not be wholly true: When demand is price inelastic, that is, when the price elasticity of demand is less than unity, increased prices can result in increased revenues. Whether increased profits obtain when inefficiencies force price increases is, of course, another matter.

10. These questions aside, a subtle difference between the first and second elements of the efficiency hypotheses should be noted. The first, organizations seek efficiency, has an individual-level counterpart: Individual persons, like organizations, are constrained to behave efficiently, and in this respect organizations may behave like lone entrepreneurs. The second, efficient organizations survive, has no individual-level counterpart because nonsurvival (as economic actors) for individual persons is not a possibility except under the most extreme conditions. Not only are organizations unlike lone entrepreneurs in this respect, but the very possibility (indeed in some instances, the option) of nonsurvival may render efficiency constraints somewhat less compelling for organizations than for individuals.

11. The hypotheses include the following: Specialist organizations are always favored in stable environments because slack or excess capacity is not needed. Generalist organizations, by contrast, are favored when environments are "coarse-grained," that is, subject to large but relatively infrequent changes. Either specialist or generalist organizations may be favored in rapidly changing "fine-grained" environments depending upon the mix of activities or "fitness set." To the extent that diverse activities are complementary, generalism is favored in fine-grained environments; to the extent that different activities are in competition, specialism is favored.

12. Some general propositions developed by Meyer and Rowan (1977) are as follows: first, with increased demands for the appearance of rationality in diverse spheres of conduct, the extensiveness of formal organization and of organizational rules and procedures increases; second, since demands for rationalization inevitably conflict, "decoupling" of organizational action from formal procedures becomes commonplace; third, inconsistencies within organiza-

tions are ignored, and a "logic of confidence and good faith" renders inspection and evaluation ritual rather than substantive.

13. See Zucker (1987a) for a review of institutional theories of organization-environment relations.

4. Performance and Persistence:
The Results of Research

Here, we review research addressing performance and persistence in organizations. First we consider tests of the efficiency model that seek causes of high performance. We then turn to some tests of the more differentiated model of organizations, specifically studies exploring concomitants of persistence. We then ask whether these research results suggest performance and persistence to have similar or different causes.

Tests of the Efficiency Model: Performance

Generally, studies assuming the efficiency model have attempted to explain organizational performance. We shall first review various performance measures and then summarize the major concomitants of performance, focusing on three sets of theoretically relevant empirical findings: (1) effects of owner versus managerial control; (2) effects of organizational structure; and (3) effects of age of firm or industry.

Measurement of performance. The underlying definition of performance is rarely explicit in research studies. Instead, performance measures are presented as the best of several imperfect indicators. Even review articles on the determinants of organizational performance (e.g., Lenz, 1981) do not define performance precisely and therefore do not consider which measures of performance best fit its underlying definition. Rather, they rely on the measures in each study,[1] which range from accounting measures of all types to perceptual measures (e.g., senior managers' assessments of profitability, see Child, 1974). Given the difficulty of defining performance, the choice of operational measures has been governed largely "on the basis of an author's particular interest or specialty" (Cunningham, 1977: 463).

To the extent that performance measures rely on different kinds of information, they are poorly correlated with one another. For example, in a study of 78 companies, the ratio of gross income to net assets was uncorrelated (.00) with percentage growth in sales (Child,

1974: 179). Moreover, top managers' perceptions of performance were inconsistently related to financial measures: Perceived profitability was highly correlated with the ratio of net income to net assets, only weakly correlated with growth in income, and not significantly correlated with growth in sales or growth in net assets (Child, 1974: 180). Early measures of performance were closely tied to production, for example, output per miner in British coal mines (Revans, 1958). The use of production measures limited comparisons between industries because different industry-specific measures could not be transformed into a common metric. As cross-industry research became more common, industry-independent, largely financial, measures of performance replaced production measures (for a review, see Weiss, 1971). Even these financial measures have evolved over time, from internal firm-centered indicators such as growth of net assets (Radice, 1971) toward external, generally market, evaluation of performance, such as return on stockholders' equity (Armour and Teece, 1978; Palmer, 1973a).

Financial measures of performance that are now commonplace are fraught with other difficulties. The internal indicators of performance, principally sales, net income, and assets, are rooted in accounting measures that are known only to approximate performance and to be applied in different ways across industries and firms. For example, one of the most commonly used measures, the ratio of net income to the book value of assets, has been shown to be systematically biased by firm size: Large firms tend to adopt accounting methods (e.g., accelerated depreciation) resulting in lower earnings than those reported by small firms (Fisher and McGowan, 1983). External performance indicators, mainly stockholders' equity, are also suspect, but for different reasons. As best as can be determined, neither prospective nor retrospective prediction of prices of individual stocks yields higher returns than does random choice. Moreover, the average gain from stock market investment since 1935 has approximately equaled the rate of inflation (Fisher and Lorie, 1977).

Because performance measures are varied and, in some instances, weakly related to one another, one might conclude that all measures of performance are imperfect and, further, that the existence of apparently high-persistence yet low-performance organizations is little more than an artifact of imperfect measurement. However, almost all of the literature on performance assumes official objectives of one sort or another, whether long-run profit maximization (in business) or attainment of program goals (for not-for-profit organizations). Other objectives are treated as dysfunctional, detracting from performance. Rarely do performance measures reflect the multiple and conflicting interests brought together in organizations. Imperfect performance measures (reflecting official objectives) are one thing, conflicting interests are another. Thus consistent with the literature, we construe performance narrowly, as measuring attainment of official objectives however imperfect.

Concomitants of performance.   The number of research studies using performance measures is staggering. For the most part, the results defy categorization. Most studies are atheoretical and, taken together, yield "laundry lists" of variables correlated with performance. These variables range from newness of plants, number of brands, and barriers to entry, generally positively related to performance, to concentration ratios and number of strike days, which are negatively related to performance (Demsetz, 1968). We shall briefly review the two most developed research areas, the effects of owner versus managerial control, and effects of firm (not market) structure. We shall also touch on one area that has received little empirical attention, the effects of organizational age on performance.[2]

Control: owner versus managerial.   Research on the impact of owner versus managerial control on firm performance has yielded mixed results. In some instances, owner-controlled firms are more profitable than are manager-controlled firms; in other instances there are no discernible differences between the two; less frequently, manager-controlled firms have been more profitable. Inconsistent results appeared most frequently in early studies of the subject.[3] Subsequent studies introduced industry-level variables in order to specify the conditions under which owner- or manager-controlled firms earn higher profits. For example, when industries were broadly grouped by overall profit rates, return on equity was very similar for the two types of control (Larner, 1970). Other variables significantly affecting owner-manager differences in performance or types of performance rewarded are monopoly power (owner-controlled firms benefit more in Palmer, 1973a), market related risk (owner-controlled firms are more risk averse than are manager-controlled firms in Palmer, 1973b, but the two types are equally risk averse in McEachern, 1975), and market power (manager-controlled firms reward size rather than profitability in McEachern, 1975).

Studies confined to a single industry find stronger relationships between owner control and profit rates (e.g., banking in Glassman and Rhodes, 1980) than cross-industry studies do, suggesting that variance across industries may obscure the relationship between control and profit. For example, in electrical engineering and textile firms, owner controlled firms showed both higher profits and higher rates of growth than did manager-controlled firms; for firms in the food industry, by contrast, managerial control leads to higher profits and growth (Radice, 1971). Overall, research evidence suggests that owner- and manager-controlled firms often pursue different objectives, profit among the former, growth among the latter, resulting in differences in financial performance between the two types, depending upon industry.[4]

Structure of the firm.   Adoption of the multidivisional structure (or M-form) may have a positive effect on performance depending on size and diversity of activities. Adoption of M-form structures in 28 petroleum companies from 1955 to 1973 was positively related to return on equity (Armour and Teece, 1978) among early adopters. A simulation study subsequently supported the superiority of the M-form over the U-form (function-based, unitary structure) in profitability, especially when the technologies involved are decomposable under decentralized decision making (Burton and Obel, 1980).

Steer and Cable (1978), using a sample from the United Kingdom, did not find that the M-form performed significantly better than did the U-form under all conditions. They found the functional U-form structure to be viable over a much broader range of organizations than was expected. The overall conclusion was that unitary organizations perform best when the firm is based in a process industry or in an uncertain environment.[5] Moreover, a recent study of the diffusion of M-form, restricted to large firms, found that adoption of the multiunit form is predicted best in the earliest historical period by variables such as related-product strategy, age of firm, and a chief executive with a sales or finance background. Over time, however, these variables lose predictive power, and the number of firms in the industry having previously adopted the M-form emerges as the best predictor of adoption by other firms (Fligstein, 1985). These results suggest that adoption of M-form structures is more a function of experience or legitimation than of efficiency gains, at least after the first wave of adoption.

Overall, relatively little evidence indicates sustained performance advantages of the multiunit form. Other causes, such as imitation, appear to be more important sources of adoption of the M-form, save perhaps for industries such as petroleum in which there are inherent efficiency gains in decentralizing operations.[6]

Age of firm. Age has not been commonly used as a variable in studies of performance because it has generally been assumed that firms show steady-state growth at a constant exponential rate until the environment changes. Only models of the "life cycle" of the firm (notably Mueller, 1972) examine age effects specifically, and these models are restricted to manager-controlled firms. Age is measured in years from the most recent innovation or other similar rejuvenating event rather than years from initial founding. Young firms are expected to show accelerating growth associated with high profitability; return on retained profits is better than could be obtained elsewhere, hence interests of managers and stockholders converge on maximum feasible growth. But as exceptional circumstances fade, profits decline and may even become negative. In mature, manager-controlled firms, rates of return on retained profits may be extremely low (Baumol et al., 1970).

Summary of empirical results.   Several qualified generalizations emerge from empirical studies of organizational performance. Owner-controlled firms are sometimes more profitable than are manager-controlled firms; managerial control is more often associated with growth. The performance of multiunit firms, particularly early adopters of the M-form, may be superior to others, but the long-term advantages of the multiunit structure are less clear. And firm performance may decline with age: There is little evidence showing firm performance, as measured by profitability, to improve steadily over time; moreover, growth usually occurs to an asymptote after which a protracted period of constant decline sets in.[7]

Tests of the Differentiated View
of Organizations: Persistence

Unlike efficiency models, models built on a more differentiated view of organizations and their environments have been operationalized in diverse ways. In this work, we are concerned specifically with concomitants of organizational persistence or longevity, and we will not consider the huge literature on organizational adaptation to changing environments.[8] We will first review measures of persistence, then turn to the major concomitants of persistence, focusing on structure and age.

Measurement of persistence.   To date, the definition of entry or birth has been treated as self-evident: the point of organizational founding. Issues raised by the life cycle theorists in economics about definition of births, specifically whether mergers, recent innovation, or similar rejuvenating events, should be treated as births, have not been directly addressed in the sociological research on persistence.[9] The problem of defining exit or death has been treated more directly. Here, the normal death is considered to be dissolution of the organization, but merger is also treated as an exit (see Freeman et al., 1983: 702-705). However, once again, there has been little attention to the measurement issues raised in the economic literature.

Concomitants of persistence.   There has been much less research on persistence than on performance, hence empirical results can be summarized quickly. Two potential causes of persistence, structure and age, have been considered. Owner versus managerial control has not been. For present purposes, we will not consider the effects of environmental elements on persistence (see especially research by Carroll, 1984b; Carroll and Delacroix, 1982; Pennings, 1982).

Structure.   One key dimension of organizational structure examined in studies of persistence is the degree of generalism versus specialism, referring to such aspects of the organization as the range of services offered and the breadth of the potential clientele. In most research, this is tied theoretically (if not operationally) to the biological idea of niche width. Generalism/specialism, heavily conditioned by characteristics of change in the local environment, has been shown to affect mortality rates of restaurants in California (Freeman and Hannan, 1983).[10] Another, quite different, approach to explaining differential rates of persistence examines the effects of the elaboration of structure on survival (Meyer et al., 1985: chap. 7). The basic argument is that proliferation of new structures—subunits and subsubunits within organizational hierarchies—advantages existing units and is therefore one of the principal causes of bureaucratic growth. In an examination of municipal agencies having finance functions in three cities in the 1890-1975 time period, Meyer and his associates demonstrate that the presence of subunits preserves the higher order unit, across both departments and divisions of the agencies (Meyer et al., 1985: 156, Table 7.1). Even controls for city, changes in administration, and historical era do not diminish the force of the original conclusion.

Age.   The basic proposition linking age with organizational persistence was first stated by Stinchcombe (1965: 148): "As a general rule, a higher proportion of new organizations fail than old. This is particularly true of new organizational forms, so that if an alternative requires new organization, it has to be much more beneficial than the old before the flow of benefits compensates for the relative weakness of the newer social structure." This idea of "liability of newness" has been tested in a wide variety of organizational settings, often with new forms:[11] the initial death rate is about five times as large as the asymptotic rate for local newspaper organizations, national labor unions, and semiconductor manufacturing firms (see Freeman et al., 1983: 702, Table 1; see also Carroll and Delacroix, 1982).

Early research on governmental organizations, however, found no empirical support for age dependence of death rates (Kaufman, 1976; Casstevens, 1980). While later research has found some evidence suggesting liability of newness, most of the age dependence was shown to be the result of heterogeneity (Meyer et al., 1985; see Barnett and Carroll, 1987: Table 2). Larger size reduces the death rate of organizations (Meyer et al., 1985: 138, Table 6.1; also Freeman et al., 1983: 705, Table 4). So do political change, historical period, and other measures of environmental context; age effects are small, at least in public bureaucracies, so that age contributes only slightly or not at all to the persistence of bureaucracies (Meyer et al., 1985: 142, Table 6.2).

Summary of empirical results.   Much less is known about concomitants of organizational persistence than of performance, as research on persistence has appeared only in the last decade. Under some conditions, generalist organizations have greater longevity than do specialists; structural complexity appears to contribute to the persistence of public bureaucracies. There is also a "liability of newness" for many organizations. Rates of organizational mortality decline with age for business firms and labor unions, although apparently not for public agencies.

Performance and Persistence: Convergence or Divergence?

We must now ask whether research suggests convergence or divergence of performance and persistence. The literature on organizational performance indicates age and managerial control under most conditions to promote low performance, and adoption of multiunit structures under some circumstances to promote high performance. The literature on organizational persistence shows age under some circumstances and complexity, whether generalism or structural differentiation, to promote high persistence. Research results with respect to age, then, suggest that the most enduring organizations may also be low performers. Performance and persistence tend to diverge in this instance. Research results with respect to organizational structure suggest no simple relationship of performance to persistence. Generalist organizations (which carry more excess capacity than do specialists) and highly differentiated organizations (which carry more administrative overhead than do undifferentiated units) have greater persistence than others have, but the performance of multiunit organizations may be superior to their unitary counterparts. Performance and persistence, thus neither converge nor diverge clearly here.

Two recent studies raise explicitly the question of whether organizational performance and persistence have similar causes. Blau's (1984) study of 152 New York architecture firms found that the same characteristics that made these firms most likely to survive the recession of the 1970s rendered them least likely to grow and increase their profits subsequently. Basically, small firms were at once most vulnerable, yet profitable, while large firms experienced greater stability at lower levels of performance. Carroll and Huo (1986) investigated the founding and mortality of just over 2,000 newspapers, as well as the over-time performance of a much smaller sample (four newspapers over 40- to 70-year time periods). Though great caution must be exercised in interpretation, both because of the small sample size and because of the use of different analytic techniques for estimating effects on founding, death, and performance, their conclusion bears repeating (Caroll and Huo, 1986: 867): "At a general level our analysis suggests that institutional environmental variables, especially political turmoil, more strongly affect the founding and death rates of organizations in the newspaper industry, whereas task environmental variables more strongly affect the performance of ongoing organizations." Since different variables affect performance

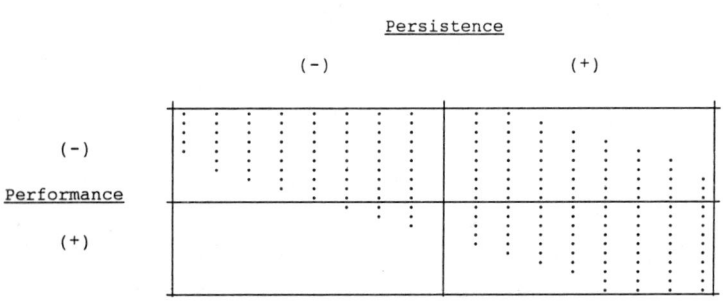

Figure 4.1   The Relationship of Performance to Persistence Revealed by Research

and persistence, it can be inferred that performance is not a strong predictor of persistence, although this is not directly tested (see Zucker, 1987c). Together, Blau's as well as Carroll and Huo's results suggest divergence of performance from persistence.

The results of research thus yield an uncertain relationship of performance to persistence. Figure 4.1 indicates that the combination of low performance and high persistence may occur in a number of instances because the most enduring organizations are, as noted, often those whose performance is weakest.

Exceptional Instances

We now turn to instances whereby economic theory acknowledges exceptions to the principle that efficient organizations survive. Three basic kinds of exceptions appear in the literature. The first suggests less than instantaneous response to low performance, an outcome of entry or exit barriers or of expectations of high future returns. The other two exceptions, declining industries and family-owned firms, are less well integrated with general economic theory and appear as lacunae. We shall first outline the economic postulates regarding mechanisms shielding firms, at least temporarily, from competitive pressure, creating a gap between performance and persistence. These mechanisms help to explain the existence of firms with low performance but not their long-term survival. We then turn to the cases of declining industries and family-owned firms. We use these two kinds of low performing, long persisting firms to illustrate mechanisms contributing to survival. We argue, however, that these exceptional instances require a theory of permanent failure in place of the ad hoc explanations offered by economists.

Exception #1: Temporary low performance. How long an interval of inefficiency, of low performance, precedes failure? The interval can be quite long in the for nonprofit organizations, many of which put survival ahead of performance.[12] The interval between low performance and failure is most immediate in taut markets, "perfectly contestable markets" (Baumol et al., 1982). But markets are seldom perfectly contestable. Entry barriers are erected to protect established firms from competition by making it difficult for new firms to enter the industry. Firms may act to create these barriers, and thus to shield themselves from competitive pressure.

It should be noted that barriers to entry can also create barriers to exit (Caves and Porter, 1977, Porter, 1976; Caves, Porter, and Spence, 1980). This is particularly the case in "committed competition" (Teece, 1981: 49), in which established firms make large and therefore irreversible commitments. Teece has argued that overinvestment may be more of a survival rather than an efficiency strategy. "Recent research on entry deterrence has identified ways in which it may pay to expand the commitment of irreversible investments in order to make entry [on the part to competitors) unfeasible. Expanding production capacity ahead of demand, advertising outlays, brand proliferation, and the like may sometimes be effective. Whether such strategies can be profitable is another matter" (Teece, 1981: 50).[13]

A second process, expectations of future profits, may sustain temporary low performance. New firms are often not profitable in the strict sense of the word, although they may have substantial assets that do not appear on the balance sheet. These assets may include human capital or control of specialized processes or products that are considered valuable if exploited.[14] Conventionally, new firms survive only a short time when the traditional balance sheet figures fail to show a profit; their mean lifespan is about three years. However, it has become increasingly evident that firms started with venture capital often are able to continue raising capital for a period well beyond three years, largely because investors believe—or express the belief—that their initial judgments will eventually prove correct.[15]

Exception #2: Declining industries.   Received economic theory tends to treat low performance as an anomalous and therefore temporary state. It has much greater difficulty with permanent low performance. Declining industries, the existence of which is acknowledged by all economists, experience permanent low performance. Even though their growth and profits are subnormal, sometimes negative, they do not fail outright.

There is an extensive literature on declining industries. Most of it is quite atheoretical, which is not surprising given economists' discomfiture with permanent low performance. Indeed, age of industry has received much more empirical attention than age of firm. A generalization formulated about 50 years ago has served as a focal point for the industry age research: "An industry tends to grow at a declining rate, its rise being eventually followed by a decline" (Burns, 1934: 171-173). Economists since 1934 have cited Burns's work as the classic and definitive study of industry development over time (see Stigler, 1947: 26; Fabricant, 1960: 52). Empirical work continues to use Burns's generalization as the starting point. However, as early as the 1960s, disconfirming empirical evidence has also been reported, leading to the conclusion that the data on which Burns's original generalization was based does not, in fact, support it. Gold (1964), updating the Burns industry series to the mid-1950s, found support for Burns's thesis for only four of 35 industries. Rather than growth to a peak, followed by decline, stable production at peak levels or a decline followed by a leveling off was the most common pattern (Gold, 1984: 59, Table 1). Restricting the Burns hypothesis to single product industries, however, provides more support for his idea, suggesting that product maturity rather than industry age accounts for decline (Gold, 1964: 63). The declining industry thesis is important because declining industries are thought to constitute a "special case" in most economic research.

Because declining industries are considered to be a special case, firms in these industries are expected to show abnormally low profit rates, unlike other firms. Hence, location in a declining industry often serves as a general explanation for profit differentials among firms. Palmer (1973a: 299), for example, noted that "Allis Chalmers and J. I. Case, producing farm implements, are in a relatively declining industry and would be expected, therefore, to report lower profit rates." Since most competition occurs within industry boundaries, it can be expected that firms in declining industries will persist despite subnormal profits. Thus in declining industries, firms persist, even though they are *expected* to experience permanent low performance.

Exception #3: Family-owned firms.   Economists have also noted that firms may have multiple goals, and that these goals may divert firms from profit maximization. Economic theory assumes that so long as firms exist in competitive environments, myriad forces compel profit maximization. Generally, multiple goals have been thought characteristic of nonprofit organizations.[16]

We would like to suggest that there are many conditions under which multiple goal problems affect for-profit firms. One case is the family-owned firm. Family business dominates in many sectors of the economy, estimated to encompass more than 90% of the 12 million businesses in the United States (Beckhard and Kyer, 1983; Pine and Mundale, 1983). Most of these are small businesses, but family-owned or family-controlled firms also constitute roughly 175 of the Fortune 500 (Lansberg, 1983). Family firms are often maintained for long periods of time after profits have eroded or vanished. For example, the Walsh family of Clinton, Illinois owned the Rock Island Southern Railway Company, an electric interurban line, and continued it for at least nine years after it ceased to be a profitable enterprise. As Hilton and Due (1964: 345) put it: "Few interurbans died a slower and more painful death than the Rock Island Southern, although the road began life with great promise."

The selection of the family business for specific exclusion from efficiency criteria rests on its peculiar mode of operation (Kepner, 1983; Calder, 1961; Ben-Prath, 1980). It clearly needs different kinds of strategies and structures, such as for the separation of business and family life and for succession of management (see Alcorn, 1982; Davis and Stern, 1980; Barry, 1975; Rosenblatt et al., 1985). The kinds of crises and conflicts also differ, and more often require some form of outside intervention to be successfully resolved (Levinson, 1974; Rosenblatt et al., 1985). Further, family businesses often become interlinked in novel ways, eschewing formal structures for exclusive use of kinship ties. Often, structures and codependencies develop between firms owned by members of the same family that differ greatly from the more commonly studied conglomerate form such as families owning both railroads and mills served by those railroads (for other examples, see Hilton and Due, 1964).

Research on family firms has stressed the unique contributions that family members can make, and the greater effort and motivation that commonly characterizes family enterprise. In only a few places is the unique contribution of the business to the family discussed: It is from the business that the family comes to draw most of its family pride, identity, inheritance, and so on. The family-run business becomes the center of family life. The firm—its success, but also its very existence—comes to define the family, as this quote from the president of a family-owned business indicates (Rosenblatt et al., 1985: 135): "What's good for the business is going to be good for the family eventually—monetary plus prestige and what have you." Family resources become commingled with company assets, often from founding; more surprising, family money may be used to cover operating expenses of businesses when they are not doing well, even to the extent of canceling family vacations (Rosenblatt et al., 1985: 146): "In order to save, say, a thousand dollars, I didn't go on a fishing trip that I planned, or a hunting trip, because the receivables were not coming in the way they are supposed to. And you can't just throw money away when you can't pay the bills."

Thus the business becomes a major source of prestige for the family, and will be maintained *even if family resources* must be used to bail out the business (Rosenblatt et al., 1985: 147): "We lost a *lot* of money . . . Until you lose money in business, unless you've done it, you really don't know what it is like. Your pride is involved." Survival of the business, thus often becomes an important goal—it is important to continue the family control, regardless of the profit motive (Marcus, 1980). For example, great reluctance is expressed if the need for, or even possibility of, selling the business arises, even if other profitable alternative investments exist (see the discussion of succession in Rosenblatt et al., 1985: chap. 10).

The Four Cases: Normal or Exceptional Instances?

We now ask whether the four cases introduced in Chapter 2 are exceptional instances of the kind identified by economists or are commonplace. Economists, it will be recalled, admit the possibility of sustained low performance in three circumstances: when anticipated future profits are expected to offset current losses, when firms are family-owned, and when firms continue operating in declining industries. These exceptional instances are treated as having distinct causes. Thus for example, firms in new and growing industries are sustained by anticipated future earnings, unprofitable family firms are sustained by "psychic income" accruing to family members, and firms in declining industries are sustained, despite diminished returns and the consequent erosion of their assets' value, by occasional small upturns in the market that yield positive profits.

We wish to point out several properties of these exceptional instances. To begin, we believe that these exceptions attribute sustained low performance to inconsistent causes. Absent current benefits to owners, firms in growing industries are maintained by expected future benefits, whereas absent expected future benefits (which drives the salvage value of assets, as used, to nearly zero), firms in declining industries are maintained by current benefits to owners. Moreover, whereas firms in growing and in declining industries are said to maximize returns to owners, family firms are said to have multiple objectives that, together, defy maximization.

Even though economists attribute these exceptional instances to inconsistent causes, we believe that elements of each of them— anticipated future benefits, multiple goals, decline—are present, in one degree or another, in most instances of permanent failure. The case of the *Los Angeles Herald Examiner* is illustrative. As an afternoon newspaper until recently, the *Herald* was in a declining industry; almost all afternoon papers in the United States have folded or merged with the rise of evening television news. And its circulation and advertising revenues remain at or near historic low levels even though it has begun morning publication. Its owners are conflicted as to whether or not the *Herald* can or should be saved: The behavior of the Hearst family indicates clearly that their multiple and divergent objectives, for example, remaining in the Los Angeles market while maintaining profitability, are blocking any dramatic decisions concerning the *Herald*. (It should be noted that individual members of the Hearst family may share these inconsistent goals.) Nonetheless, at least some of the *Herald Examiner's* owners and management remain persuaded that future profitability is possible—somehow. Absent this belief, whether or not it had any basis in fact, continued publication of the *Herald* would be difficult.

Like the *Herald,* Rath Packing also operated in an industry that was declining, owing partly to shrunken markets and partly to extreme cost pressures. By the time workers assumed effective control of the firm, Rath's business had slipped to half of what it had been in the late 1950s. And worker control caused multiple and divergent goals to surface at Rath. Clearly, worker ownership was an end in itself, apart from profitability, for many of Rath's employees. But worker control, it turned out, did not ensure harmonious labor relations: The management team installed by workers pursued production and cost-control objectives that ultimately triggered picketing and a small strike. These differences notwithstanding, plans for rescuing and resuscitating Rath abounded until the last days of its existence; future profits remained a possibility, albeit a hypothetical one, throughout.

The case of Cathedral High School is somewhat different from either the *Herald Examiner* or Rath Packing. Cathedral High itself was not in decline at the time its sale was negotiated, although other Los Angeles diocesan high schools were. The Archdiocese wished to close Cathedral precisely because its assets were extraordinarily valuable compared to other schools; it was frustrated in this effort when, through political action, the value of Cathedral's property was reduced to essentially zero. As in the cases of the *Herald* and Rath, multiple and divergent goals among the actors affiliated with Cathedral High rendered closing the school impossible. The archdiocese stood to gain considerably from selling the property. The Christian Brothers, who stood to gain nothing from the sale, publicly accused the archdiocese's lobbyists of lying to the Los Angeles City Council and privately threatened to sue the archdiocese for defamation. Various politicians seized upon the threatened closing of Cathedral High as a Hispanic issue; ultimately, Mayor Tom Bradley sided with supporters of the school and presented Cathedral with a $100,000 check from an "anonymous donor," to be used to rehabilitate the campus. It goes without saying that those who fought the sale of Cathedral High believed its future, as a school, to be assured; positive future returns, educationally if not financially, were expected. At the time, no one, including the archdiocese, anticipated that Cathedral's enrollments would decline shortly.

The fourth case, that of U.S. steel companies, combines elements of the first three cases. Steel, to begin, was (and remains) a declining industry. The stated objectives of steel management diverged substantially from the wishes of the surrounding community. Executives sought short-term profitability (or minimally, recovery), to be achieved through massive contraction of the industry. The community, indeed, a region encompassing three states, sought to prevent collapse of their economies and dislocation of their citizens through modernization rather than contraction. Both the firms and the surrounding communities believed that their strategies would provide a long-term solution to the decline of steel. What distinguishes the case of the steel industry from the three other cases is the magnitude of the problem and the ensuing conflict, and the involvement of governmental authorities and political organizations beyond the local level.

How, one might ask, can long-run decline, multiple goals, yet expectations of positive future returns exist together in the same setting? Clearly, they cannot so long as only the rational, calculated aspects of behavior are considered, and so long as actors' preferences or utilities are similar such that rational calculation yields the same choices for all. But allowing apparently nonrational elements and differences in actors' preferences to enter the picture suggests several possible explanations. One is the psychology of commitment, another is loyalist behavior, a third is a process known as goal succession in organizations. The first, the psychology of commitment, is observed when repeated failure of a policy actually increases actors' public commitment to it (Staw, 1976). The second, loyalist behavior, describes the conduct of actors who choose deliberately to remain in a declining firm rather than exit it in the belief that their best efforts within the organization will lead to improvement (Hirschman, 1970). The third, goal succession, is observed when organizations, having attained a specific goal (Sills, 1957) or having found their stated goals unattainable (Cyert, 1978), determine a new set of objectives to be pursued. The similarities of these three should be kept in mind: Each is a response to organizational decline, failure, or low performance. But their differences are important. Public commitment creates inflexibility and, by implication, predictions of positive future returns so long as present policies are pursued. Goal succession, by contrast, implies the expectation that past policies would have yielded zero future returns had they not been altered. Loyalist behavior occupies an intermediate position between commitment and goal succession, a position anticipating positive future outcomes provided that the correct choices are made—without specifying what these choices are.

These mechanisms are similar in that each is a response to decline. They diverge in anticipating very different future states for the organization. It is precisely for this reason, we believe, that decline triggers uncertainty of a sort that is not experienced during intervals of growth. And it is for the same reason, we believe, that decline is often a protracted process in which initial low performance gives way to sustained low performance or permanent failure. Let us put the matter somewhat more concretely: People respond differently to the initial stages of organizational decline, leaving some committed to past policies, some committed to the organization but not to specific policies, and some intent on changing the organization or leaving it. Considerable uncertainty is created, yielding a prolonged interval of decline.

The reader might ask why a theory of permanent failure need go beyond the notion that commitment, loyalist behavior, and succession of goals may arise simultaneously in periods of low performance. The reason is straightforward: These principles of individual behavior do not specify which actors in and around organizations remain committed to the past, which actors are loyalists, and which actors are most willing to change. To anticipate the discussion in the next chapter, we argue that permanent failure arises most often when three circumstances obtain: First, low performance occurs, perhaps because of exogenous causes; second, owners or their equivalents having legal control over organizations attempt to implement changes aimed at restoring performance, or, more commonly, attempt to redeploy capital to other more profitable arenas; and third, these changes are resisted effectively by others in and around organizations because they are less concerned than are owners about financial performance (or, more generally, official objectives) but are, at the same time, dependent on the organization for other benefits, including wages (for workers), dues-paying membership (for unions), goods and services (for customers), and the organization's contribution to the local economy (for political leaders). Dependence relations among these actors rather than their individual psychological predispositions, we argue, are ultimately responsible for patterns of permanent failure.

In sum, economic theory acknowledges the possibility of high-persistence, low-performance organizations, but only as exceptional instances. This approach presents two sorts of difficulties. One, already mentioned, is that these instances demonstrate the relationship of performance to persistence to be weak, at least under certain circumstances, and are inconsistent with the general principle that efficient, high performing organizations survive. Another difficulty, equally serious, is that the explanation of each of these instances is ad hoc. To illustrate: Temporary low performance is sustained by rational strategies of owners who erect entry barriers, but it is also sustained by highly uncertain (in the sense that they cannot be calculated) expectations of positive future returns; permanent low performance is an outcome of inertia and the "winding down" of obsolete industries, but it is also the result of multiple and inconsistent objectives of family-owned firms. No consistent utility maximization on the part of owners (or, for that matter, on the part of anyone else) operates in these explanations, nor do any nonrational elements operating consistently. Some alternative and more consistent explanation of low performance is therefore needed.

We wish to propose that these exceptional instances can be understood in the context of a general theory of permanently failing organizations. The elements of the theory are straightforward and derived more from the differentiated view of organizations and their environments than from economic models. The basic notion, which will be elaborated next, is that multiple interests and motivations rather than the untrammeled pursuit of official objectives drive the behavior of most organizations; that these interests and motivations sometimes place the preservation of the organization ahead of these objectives, sometimes for dependent actors and owners alike; and that, even absent formal authority, actors who are dependent upon organizations are often motivated to assert their preference for existing organizational patterns in the face of proposals for change.

Notes

1. There are a handful of studies that do define performance, but unfortunately in vague or inconsistent ways. Theoretical treatments are sometimes more forthcoming. Caves (1980: 64), for example, defines "economic performance of the firm" as "its efficiency

(measured by the divergence of its input-output relation from the best attainable), its profitability relative to comparable competitors, or some other operational test of efficiency."

2. We explicitly exclude from consideration here the literature on market structure and performance, because it both strays away from our central interests in this monograph and has not uncovered strong empirical relationships (see Weiss, 1971, and Vernon, 1972, for excellent reviews). The large literature on size and profitability is also not reviewed here (see Crum, 1939; McConnell, 1945; Osborn, 1951; Steckler, 1963; Hall and Weiss, 1967; Marcus, 1969; Demsetz, 1973). Very few studies include any measure of firm age, and thus move away from our topic; this may explain in part the mixed results found in studies of size and profitability.

3. See Kamerschen, 1968; Monsen et al., 1968. However, both of these studies rely on profit measures that are systematically biased by the fact, noted previously, that different depreciation methods tend to be adopted by management-controlled and owner-controlled firms.

4. Useem (1980: 50) reports strong effects of any amount of ownership, even relating minor stock positions. However, he reviews only studies in the largest U.S. companies. He reports *incorrectly* that the "profit performance of owner and manager controlled firms do not materially differ.

5. This result is not necessarily inconsistent with Williamson's (1975) argument that transaction costs determine organizational form, which states merely that firms adopt the most efficient forms. See also Williamson and Bhargava (1972). Thompson (1981) has argued that the strength of the Steer and Cable results can be attributed to the very poor performance of the holding company form (H-form) during the period of their study, and hence are in part artifactual.

6. It may be that performance is more a function of the internal consistency of the organizational form selected than of the choice of a particular form. In a study of the airline industry, Child (1977) found that the low performers were most often firms whose structures were not fully consistent with either M- or U-form.

7. These issues have received little attention in the nonprofit and government sectors, first because performance measurement is

seldom attempted, and second because form of control has lower variance.

8. This literature is reviewed in Pfeffer (1982) and Scott (1987). Changes in task environment do not appear to alter persistence though changes in the institutional environment do (Carroll and Huo, 1986; Zucker, 1987c).

9. Mergers do not normally occur because the acquired company is failing but because its shares are undervalued relative to underlying assets or expected sales (Boyle, 1970; Melicher and Rush, 1974).

10. The effects of generalism versus specialism were compared in fine-grained environments, in which change occurs incrementally, and in coarse-grained environments, in which change occurs in large steps. Freeman and Hannan, it should be noted, defined grain as seasonality of demand for individual restaurants, whereas environmental variability was defined as the rate of change in restaurant sales in an entire community. Somewhat consistent with their predictions, Freeman and Hannan found death rates of generalist organizations to be higher than of specialist organizations (in which broad menu defined generalist, and ethnic or narrow-range menu defined specialist) in fine-grained environments. In fine-grained environments, generalists had lower death rates. These results, however, held only in environments in which variability—again, change in community restaurant sales—was high.

11. Measures of age, it should be noted, have been exclusively at the organizational level in studies of persistence. Virtually no attention has been paid to industry age.

12. Cyert (1978) notes that universities have developed explicit policies for managing decline.

13. Barriers are thought to operate also within industries, in which groups of firms arise owing to specialized capabilities, market characteristics, and transactions. Similarly specialized firms tend to have informal lines of communication and collusion, with mobility barriers separating the various groups of firms from each other (Caves, 1984).

14. We are indebted to David Teece for suggesting this source of nonprofitability of new firms and the inadequacy of balance sheet figures for understanding it.

15. A recent *Los Angeles Times* (February 22, 1986: IV-1) article illustrates this principle: "The fortunes of Newport Pharmaceuticals are tied exclusively to Isoprinosine, and the company has paid dearly for putting all its eggs in one basket. Until last year, the company had posed losses for each of its 18 years in business . . . . Through the years . . . [it] has unsuccessfully sought [FDA] approval for use of Isoprinosine—its only product—for a variety of ailments, from herpes to hepatitis."

16. Clarkson (1972: 366), for example, notes that, "the personnel of nonproprietary hospitals do not face an all-encompassing overriding criterion such as the wealth maximization rule. . . . The reasons for becoming nonproprietary nonprofit-seeking are varied—the organizers may find different aspects or outcomes of organization under private property rights undesirable."

5. Toward a Theory
of Permanent Failure

A theory of organizational maintenance under conditions of low performance, we believe, must accomplish several purposes. First, such a theory must extend the explanation of organizational maintenance beyond the exceptional circumstances already acknowledged by economists. Second, the theory must explain why organizations whose performance has deteriorated do not easily escape from low performance, yet are not easily displaced. We do not seek to explain exogenous causes of low performance; they are beyond the purview of this book.[1] Nor do we seek to explain all instances of organizational persistence or inertia. We seek instead to explain how low performance can trigger forces favoring maintenance of organizations. A theory of permanent failure must, finally, explain the combination of high persistence and low performance as the outcome of something more than the rational pursuit of ownership interests (or their equivalents, in nonprofit organizations). Since by definition, low performance does not contribute to ownership interests in firms and in many non-profit organization, we shall argue that organizational maintenance under conditions of low performance must be an outcome of other forces.

A Model of Permanent Failure

Under what conditions will performance be only one of many constraints, and not necessarily determinative of survival? In conventional theorizing, the motivation for maintaining organizations has been (in the case of firms) profit, the benefits of which accrue to owners or shareholders, or (in the case of public agencies) performance of specific functions, the benefits of which accrue to the commonweal. A broader conception of who benefits from maintaining organizations is needed, however. Those who benefit are not restricted to persons having legal ownership or control of an organization but may also encompass workers, suppliers, customers, and members of the surrounding community who, lacking ownership or sovereign rights, may be regarded as dependent upon the organization. These dependent actors benefit more from the main-

TABLE 5.1
Implications of Motivation and Power
for the Relation of Performance to Persistence

Motivation	Who Benefits	Means	Relation of Performance to Persistence
performance	owners/residual claimants	efficiency	performance → persistence
mixed	managers	"management"	performance →? persistence
organizational maintenance	dependent actors	(see Table 5.2)	performance decoupled from persistence

tenance of an organization than from its performance because they have no claims on profits or on other benefits associated with attainment of official objectives.[2] This, of course, is an analytic distinction—in actual organizations, especially those operating in the nonprofit sector, differences among the interests of dependent actors may be more significant.

Motivation and organizational maintenance.   To build a model explaining the maintenance of organizations, we need to consider both *motivations* to continue an organization in the face of declining performance and the *power* to do so. We shall consider mainly the case of firms, but a parallel argument could be made for nonprofit and public organizations. We shall consider the motivations and power of owners, managers, and dependent actors.

As indicated in Table 5.1, owners of firms are generally motivated by financial performance, which is sought by allocating resources to their most efficient uses. High performing units will be sustained, while resources will be drained from units whose performance is substandard. A close correspondence of performance to persistence is expected, other things being equal.

The motivation of managers is somewhat more complex. To the extent that managers are rewarded for profitability, they are motivated to improve performance. However, to the extent that managers' skills are not transferable to other settings, they are dependent upon the firm and thus motivated to maintain it, in fact motivated to expand it regardless of the effects of growth on profitability (Radice, 1971). Under conditions of declining or chronically low performance, these dual motivations yield an uncertain relationship of performance to persistence, assuming managers have the power to influence decisions as to whether or not to maintain organizations. Table 5.1 indicates that the motivation of managers is somewhat mixed, that their mixed motives lead managers to pursue "good management" rather than unalloyed efficiency, and that the combination of mixed motives and uncertain power of managers renders the connection of performance to persistence weakened, compared to owners.

Performance and persistence should be almost perfectly related in the first case, and only slightly less closely related in the second. What then accounts for the tendency of performance and persistence to diverge, causing the creation of a large group of permanently failing organizations? We need to ask, in other words, who benefits from maintenance of an organization that does not generate financial returns commensurate with other investments. In seeking the answer, we draw from social psychological understanding of dependence: Those who are dependent on an organization have few alternatives to it and therefore continue to benefit from its existence independently of its performance. Moreover, the fewer the alternatives, the more dependent these actors are (Emerson, 1962; Thibaut and Kelly, 1959), and thus the greater their motivation to maintain the organization regardless of its performance.

Workers, who receive solely wage or salary compensation; the community, which receives only the side benefits of firm operation in the form of employment, purchasing power, and access to goods and services produced by the firm; and the organizations using the firm's products as inputs, requiring the firm's services, or selling their products to the firm, are in a position of dependency and therefore have the motivation to support the maintenance of the firm apart from its efficiency and resulting performance. This motivation is relatively constant, hence, as indicated in Table 5.1, it weakens the relation of performance to persistence.

Under conditions of high performance, motivation to maintain the organization is shared by both owners and residual claimants, on the one hand, and dependent actors on the other, though it tends to be somewhat higher for the owners. The motivation to maintain the organization stems from somewhat different sources; for owners and residual claimants, it is positive returns, while for dependent actors it is, as already indicated, jobs, customer and supplier relationships, and the economic well-being of the community. Of course, this rests on a comparative assessment of alternatives, as portfolio theory explicitly suggests for owners, and as the job search literature assumes for workers. Under conditions of low performance, however, positive returns vanish, and owners and residual claimants lose motivation to maintain the organization.[3] The same does not hold for dependent actors. Indeed, some conditions *causing* performance to deteriorate, such as above-normal wages, "rents" of office, and the failure of other firms in the same industry (during a normal decline), limit alternatives available to dependent actors and actually increase their motivation to maintain the organization.

Figure 5.1 graphically depicts how relative motivation to maintain the organization diverges as one moves from high to low performance. The solid line shows owners and residual claimants' motivation declining sharply with performance. The broken line shows dependent actors' motivation as essentially constant, other things being equal. It is important to note that the relative level of dependent actors' motivation to maintain the organization, and hence the exact position of the dotted line, will depend upon the alternatives available to them. If they have above-normal wages, for example, the alternatives will decrease, and the overall level of motivation to maintain the firm should increase. In any case, as performance declines, the motivation of dependent actors to maintain the firm increases in strength, relative to that of owners and residual claimants.

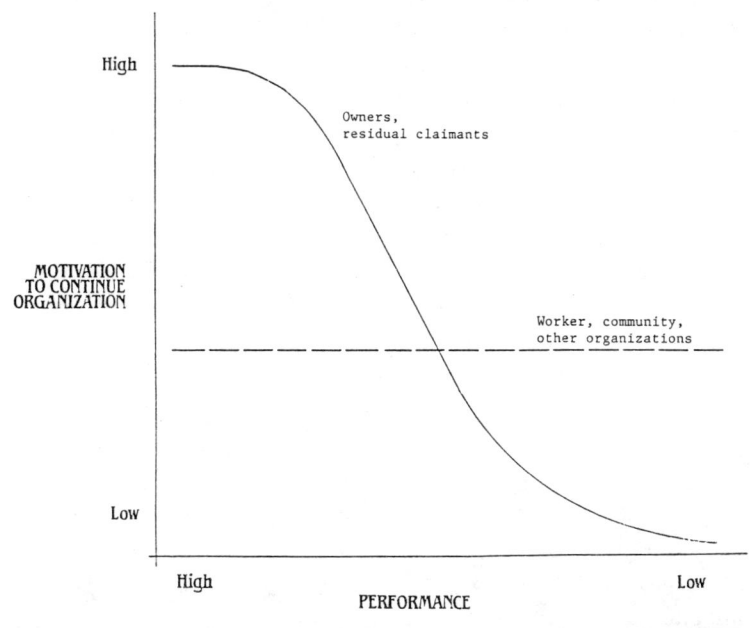

Figure 5.1 Motivation to Maintain Organization as a Function of Performance

Motivation and risk.   A simple model illustrates the process of permanent failure when organization is valued apart from its performance properties. Figure 5.2 reproduces the familiar fourfold table displaying the relationship of performance to persistence. The figure illustrates the alternatives available to permanently failing organizations whose performance is low but has not deteriorated to the point that its existence is immediately threatened. The arrow pointing from the upper right to the lower right quadrant indicates that improved performance, or success, is one possibility. Another possibility, indicated by the horizontal arrow pointing to the upper left quadrant, is diminished persistence, or outright failure.

Other things being constant, particularly wages, all actors associated with an organization can be assumed to share a preference for improved performance over diminished persistence, for success over failure. *But permanently failing organizations do not choose*

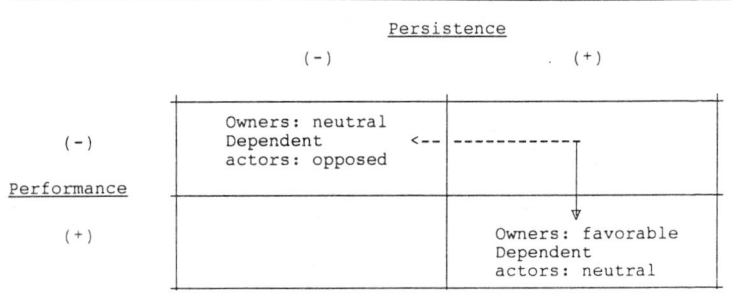

Figure 5.2   Paths from Permanent Failure

simply between success and failure. They choose instead whether or not to pursue success—and thereby to risk failure. The costs and benefits of strategies aimed at relieving permanent failure differ dramatically, depending upon the relative value of performance and of organization, again, apart from its performance properties. For owners, improved performance promises positive returns, and diminished persistence is essentially costless given that performance is already low. Risky strategies may, therefore, be acceptable.[4] For others who value organization, improved performance offers limited gains, but outright failure is costly, sometimes catastrophic. Thus, even though there may be consensus that performance is low and should be improved, only risk-free means toward this end are acceptable to actors valuing organization, and these actors will seek to limit the alternatives available to actors valuing performance and therefore willing to pursue risky strategies. Permanent failure thus is an outcome of divergent preferences among the actors associated with an organization or, in some instances, ambivalence on the part of individual actors.[5] In either case, choices leading potentially either to success or to failure may be blocked, and temporary low performance gives way to permanent failure.

Two further comments should be made. First, the model sketched in Figure 5.2 does not explain why organizations perform poorly in the first place. It explains only why they fail to escape from substandard performance quickly. Second, the model assumes no one to be lazy.[6] The vigorous pursuit of self-interest can give rise to permanent failure resulting from the organization's incapacity to choose strategies offering the possibility of outright success, but risking outright failure. Third, we recognize that, absent resources, no organization can continue (Yuchtman and Seashore, 1967). Past a point, owners' motivation *not* to maintain an organization may be so strong as to overcome almost all countervailing forces. Substandard performance, however, does not render an organization bereft of resources, at least in the short run.

Motivation and power.   Before beginning our discussion of power, the basic argument bears repeating: Dependent actors—individual workers, communities, and other organizations—value organization apart from performance. As performance declines, their motivation to maintain the organization becomes relatively greater than that of owners or residual claimants (refer again to Figure 5.1). At this point, performance and persistence begin to diverge dramatically. To the extent that organization is valued, these interested parties will seek to avoid risky choices, which might improve performance, but which also might cause outright failure.

Economists consider those dependent on the firm to have little power to influence it. This view is generally mirrored in the sociological literature, with some notable exceptions such as Mechanic (1962). However, the power of dependent (and therefore apparently powerless) actors has been central to the study of national revolutions, to the study of power relations in social psychology and in community research, and to work on collective behavior. Because the literatures themselves are tangential to our argument, we will not review them here; rather, we will borrow concepts from them, simply noting our sources. As shown in Table 5.2, there are conceptually four ways in which the joining of interests with actions can give rise to influence over decision making in organizations. Note that individual actors are the unit of analysis in the upper leftmost cell of Table 5.2, whereas groups are the units in the other cells. The table describes conditions giving rise to effective power of individuals and groups, since neither individuals (owners) nor groups (dependent actors) can act successfully without power.

Interests, the horizontal axis of Table 5.2, refers to the objectives sought by actors and may be fully divergent, with no overlap across actors, or exhibit varying degrees of commonality up to the point of complete convergence. Examples of divergent interests include owners attempting to maintain profitability, while a union is attempting to maintain jobs, and, somewhat less oppositional, individual workers who are union members participating on the basis of very different interests such as high wages or job security (which themselves under some conditions are incompatible objectives, although they need not be). An example of convergent interests might be the local legislative bodies and the courts: Legislators may support the maintenance of rail service to provide jobs for their constituents, while statutes restricting rail abandonments or making abandonments difficult on grounds of public welfare (i.e., the idea that some minimum level of public conveyances must be maintained) may lead the courts to order the railroad company to continue operations. Though the actions of legislatures and courts have very different rationales, the consequences of their actions, in this case, converge on the same outcome of maintaining rail service.

Separable from interests, action refers to the degree of coordination among actors, and may range from completely independent, whereby individual actors have little knowledge of or influence over what other parties are doing, to joint activity, whereby the action of any one party is completely contingent on the action of the others. Examples of independent actors include owners, who generally negotiate with unions separately and who seldom coalesce (trade associations aside, and these are limited in the United States), and groups such as the community organizations and the courts who normally have very different agendas but may converge on a single issue. Examples of joint action include coalitions of individual actors (e.g., in unions) who, despite very different interests, realize that coordinated action is the only effective response to power exercised by owners. Joint action is generally planned and very deliberate when interests diverge. In sharp contrast, when interests converge, joint

TABLE 5.2
Types of Influence over Decision Making

| | Interests | |
	Diverge	Converge
Independent	means: direct power actors: owners action: exercise ownership preregotatives model: theory of firm 1.	means: issue-focused pressure actors: unrelated groups action: redefine ownership prerogatives model: revolution 4.
Joint	means: group formation actors: dependent individuals action: oppose ownership initiatives model: power of dependents 2.	means: coordinated action actors: interrelated groups action: community-wide mobilization model: resource mobilization 3.

Action

Cases:

Cell 1:   Herald Examiner
Cell 2:   Rath Packing
Cell 3:   Cathedral High School
Cell 4:   Steel closings

action *on any single issue* may be somewhat planned and structured, but the same coalition will not tend to reform around other issues.

To simplify presentation, action and interests are dichotomized in Table 5.2. Each cell in Table 5.2 indicates the type of influence that is expected to be used, the individuals or groups most likely to use each type, the means that are most likely to be employed, and the relevant social science literature bearing on each type of influence. In the upper rightmost cell of Table 5.2, where interests diverge and action is independent, only individual persons exercise power effectively; hence, the most powerful actors are likely to be owners or residual claimants. (When the organization is located in the public sector, or is heavily regulated, the state may replace the owners as the most powerful actor.) Dependent actors, to the extent that their interests diverge and their actions are independent, are not expected to have an impact on decision making. Under most conditions the individual community members or individual workers do not have the power to influence decisions concerning termination of business (Metzgar, 1980).

Let us now review the different kinds of permanent failure suggested in each of the cells of Table 5.2. Cell 1, the upper leftmost quadrant of the table, illustrates permanent failure through indecision or faulty decisions. The other three cells in the table suggest structural rather than individual processes leading to organizational maintenance under conditions of low performance, giving rise to permanent failure. The processes identified in cells 2, 3, and 4 rest primarily on the formation or use of group structures, since individual action on the part of dependent actors is rarely effective.[7] And all three processes have in common the displacement of elites or elite interests by nonelites or their interests. The possibility that interests of elite owners may be subordinated to interests of nonelite dependent actors is widely recognized in macrosociology, but it is rarely considered in organizational theory or organizational economics. It is of some significance for the present discussion, however, because when coupled with the observation, sketched here, that low performance causes interests of elite owners to diverge from the interests of nonelite dependents, a complete theory of permanent failure becomes possible. We will move about the table counter-clockwise.

Cell 1.   Family firms, such as the Los Angeles Herald Examiner, illustrate the kind of permanent failure that is typical of cases falling in the upper leftmost cell of Table 5.2. Here, permanent failure occurs through indecision on the part of owners and, indeed, the *Herald Examiner* has been maintained for more than 10 years of unprofitable operation. Other family firms have faced similar choices, but not always with the same outcome. A Harvard Business School case, "Springs Mills: Textile Manufacturing" illustrates the point.[8] The family ownership built new mills and pursued a good-neighbor policy, not even closing mills or laying off employees during the Great Depression. But when Springs Mills went public in 1966, a new "get-tough policy" was initiated by its first nonfamily CEO. "His yardstick: a division must earn 10 per cent profit after taxes or it goes, either through sale or outright liquidation" (*New York Times*, 1979). Under these guidelines, some plants have been sold, others closed. The worker and community orientation of the firm when it was family owned is still mentioned (see the preceding Harvard Business School case) but it is clear that profitability is the most important criterion with permanent failure not tolerated, not even for the sake of humanitarian concerns.

Cell 2. The type of permanent failure falling into cell 2 of Table 5.2 is illustrated by examples ranging from unionization to employee ownership of companies, one instance of the latter being the case of Rath Packing. Here, workers coalesced about a plan for employee ownership, exercising the power of dependents. The poor financial condition of Rath in conjunction with the availability of federal funds to worker-controlled firms made it advantageous for stockholders to support employee ownership through dilution of their own holdings. But employee ownership yielded no palpable benefits—certainly no returns to stockholders—other than keeping Rath alive for a period of time. The $23 million loss in the eight years preceding employee ownership was eclipsed by the $40 million loss incurred from 1981 through 1985. All told, Rath continued in operation with substantial losses in 12 of its last 13 years (deferred wages and pensions produced the one profit), an excellent example of protracted failure without the expected shutdown. Clearly, credit for maintaining the company during its last five years goes to the dependent actors, the workers who became the owners of Rath.

In cell 2 of Table 5.2, where interests diverge but action is joint, the actors coalesce because of a common desire to block the power of the owners. This view of power-increasing coalitions comes from the power-dependence exchange framework (Emerson, 1962): The power of A over B is equal to, and based upon, the dependence of B over A. A corollary of Emerson's exchange theory is that the dependence of A upon B is directly proportional to the importance of goals mediated by B, and inversely proportional to the availability of suppliers outside the A-B relationship.[9] Emerson suggests several mechanisms to reduce dependence and thereby reduce power inequalities. One, formation of coalitions among dependent actors such that the more powerful party is confronted by a group with the ability to act in a unified way, applies with force to the case of permanently failing organizations.[10] Emerson's resolution, then, asserts that if the (possibly differing) interests—unified primarily by dependence on a more powerful other—coalesce in joint action, then the collective power to influence decisions of the other will increase.

Since interests are divergent in the lower leftmost cell of Table 5.2, coalitions will tend to form around issues for which some degree of common interest exists, though the underlying interests remain divergent. In the case of union formation, perhaps the best known example (Zucker, 1987b), workers unite around a very small number of issues, abandoning issues for which agreement is weak in the work force, such as working conditions specific to a craft that is a small minority of the firm's workers. It is important to note that the impact of unionization on the maintenance of low performing organizations is both indirect, through high wages and contract provisions limiting "outsourcing," and direct, through political action opposing plant closures.

In the case of employee ownership of companies, individual interests also diverge but, as with unionization, lead to joint action that serves directly to maintain low performing firms. Interests that lead workers to participate in employee buy outs range from simple job retention to ownership goals and even employee participation as an end in itself. These interests are so varied there is no single explanation of participation, accounting for contradictory findings in the research literature. Several studies have found that workers already unemployed (or unable to engage in search) and unable to find alternative jobs have high motivation to participate in employee buy outs in order to regain their old jobs (Hammer and Stern, 1980; Stern and Hammer, 1978; Shirom, 1972). Other studies have found propensity for risk-taking to be a significant predictor (Cosyns and Loveridge, 1981). Still other research has found entrepreneurial and collective participation in decision making to be among the principal motives of workers (Stern et al., 1979; Bernstein, 1980). These studies focus on the (somewhat contradictory) worker interests that would be served by a buy out, but fail to consider whether financial resources necessary to purchase the company are available to workers. Indeed, one set of studies found those most likely to favor buy outs are the unemployed.

Given the varied interests apparent in previous research, how can workers engage in coordinated action? A recent study puts all of these variables into perspective by showing that they *jointly* determine worker decisions to participate in a buy out. Buy out decisions by individual employees of a supermarket chain facing a shutdown were significantly affected by desire for ownership, propensity for risk taking, desire for worker participation, annual income (a measure of ability to participate in a buy out), and unemployment status (Hochner and Granrose, 1985: Tables 2 and 4). Despite this range of interests, workers were able to engage in coordinated action; the buy out was successfully accomplished, and some of the stores reopened as employee-owned and operated. Divergent interests, then, are still able to produce joint action, even in the face of substantial barriers: "Establishing employee ownership has been an unusual collective action because employee ownership requires a difficult, large scale mobilization of many people, rather than action by a few union leaders" (Hochner and Granrose, 1985: 863).

Cell 3.   The two rightmost cells in Table 5.2 examine the effects of actors dependent on the organization when interests converge. In the lower rightmost cell of Table 5.2, collective action occurs when interests converge and joint, coordinated action takes place. The case of Cathedral High School in Los Angeles provides an illustration of collective action. There was a strong economic argument for selling Cathedral's property and moving its students to the underenrolled diocesan churches in the vicinity. But the community would not let Cathedral High be sold. The protest began with the teachers, drawn from the Christian Brothers, who were not consulted about the sale, the alumni, and many distinguished members of the local Hispanic community; and it continued with the Los Angeles City Council declaring a one-year building moratorium for the study of the development proposed for the land, a subsequent council vote to declare the school a cultural monument, and a lawsuit, filed by alumni and other concerned citizens, to stop the transaction, calling it an illegal transfer of land. With coordinated action among these groups, the sale of Cathedral High's property was finally halted. Of greater long-term significance, perhaps, is the impact of community action on subsequent decisions of the archdiocese: There is now extreme reluctance to entertain the possibility of closing any school, no matter how low its enrollments.

Research on collective action has focused on the process through which groups mobilize resources. Identification of the resources to be mobilized often occurs after the fact, and for this reason, theoretical development has proceeded slowly. Most research has stressed internal movement resources (e.g., Tilly, 1978). In the case of Cathedral High School, internal resources might include such elements as leadership and organizing skills of students, staff, and alumni. It is unlikely, however, that these resources alone could have sustained Cathedral High. Mobilization of external resources seems to be especially crucial.[11] Generally, the availability and strategic posture of potential alliance partners appears to be essential to effective collective action (Tarrow, 1983: chap. 3), particularly if the community has stable and extensive interorganizational networks (see Aiken and Alford, 1970). Specifically in the case of Cathedral High, actions taken by the Hispanic community and elected Los Angeles officials seem to have made the difference between continuing and closing the school.

Some additional conditions affect the likelihood of collective action: Resource mobilization is likely to be effective to the extent that an organization has reciprocal dependencies that limit its autonomy of action. For example, a voluntary organization may be dependent on community support; if closure of a subunit were proposed, then the community could threaten to withdraw its support of the remaining organizational units. Effective resource mobilization is also likely to the extent that an organization is unable to relocate the rest of its operations, perhaps because of sunk costs or special natural resources, such as water rights, or people with specialized skills located in the community. For example, engineers with specialized knowledge, training, and contacts within the semiconductor field are located in particular areas of the country, especially Silicon Valley and Route 128 in Boston.

Cell 4. Let us turn, finally, to the upper rightmost cell in Table 5.2. In this cell, when interests converge but action is independent, the desired outcome is generally change in ownership prerogatives. Actors are typically several independent groups: Owing to differences in objectives, varied socioeconomic backgrounds of members, or even legal requirements for independence (as in the courts), they do not coalesce to act jointly. The case of shutdowns in the steel industry illustrates the form of permanent failure associated with convergent interests absent joint action. To be sure, some groups coalesced and others were formed as the steel valley revolt spread. But, as indicated in Chapter 2, no single strategy guided the action of diverse groups. Quite the opposite, action was often uncoordinated. Those groups favoring boycott of steel firms (and of their banks), those groups attempting to maintain marginal steel plants under private control, and those groups favoring public takeover of seizure of the steel mills clearly had disparate agendas.

Convergence increases total power by combining the effects of otherwise unconnected groups, for example, workers who wish to retain their jobs and the federal government that wishes to promote national security—judged to be harmed by closing a defense contractor. This intersection of group interests, if it occurs on a large scale, may be sufficient to redefine ownership prerogatives. As the literature on national revolutions indicates, action may be effective without coordination or cohesion: Societies can be changed in revolutionary ways by the simple convergence of forces ("workers," "elites," "peasants," each operating separately). These individuals and groups, even when highly organized internally, do not coalesce, but pursue their own interests and goals in a way that converges on the intended outcome of change in the prevailing social order.[12]

Convergent interests absent joint action have occurred in other organizational settings, for example in response to proposed abandonments of rail service to small communities.[13] Here, workers are normally interested in maintaining service because of potential job losses; some organizations in the community might be wholly dependent on the railroad for movement of goods or raw materials, and the entire community may be concerned about its viability should business brought to the community by the railroad be lost. According to convergence theory, these interests may facilitate each other without any formal coalescence or organization. The reasons for pursuing the same objective—continuation of rail service—differ, but if each group acts independently, the forces converge on organizational maintenance.

The fact that these groups act independently points to the single-issue character of most action in the upper rightmost cell of Table 5.2. Convergence proceeds on an issue-by-issue basis, with the primary goal of power sought in a single specific decision context. Hence, the probability of a second instance of convergence by the same mix of groups around another issue is small. For example, local and state communities acted to provide financial support for Chrysler suppliers and subsidiaries—beyond the national bailout—aligning themselves temporarily with unions concerned with preserving jobs. The need to keep the local plants in operation caused the communities and unions to converge on this issue; the convergence, however, was generally limited to this issue of organizational maintenance. The groups went their separate ways when faced with other unrelated issues.[14]

Sometimes these actions are contemporaneous, but actions appear to be more effective when they are extended over a lengthy period of time, with groups acting sequentially or with minimal overlap to block closure of a plant or termination of service. Sometimes these actions are largely independent, as in the upper rightmost cell of Table 5.2, but sometimes they become more coordinated through systematic mobilization of resources, as in the lower rightmost cell of Table 5.2. For example, local government may intervene first to attempt to maintain the firm; when they are not successful, local government officials may appeal to legislative bodies or the courts that would require the firm to stay in business. Particularly when the firm is in a regulated industry, this strategy mobilizes interests very different from those of the owner, and seeks to activate the interests of other groups in a way that will produce maintenance of the firm by providing the control agent with the necessary information to permit sanctioning (Zald, 1978: 90-92). Interurban electric railways again provide numerous examples, including the maintenance of the north shoreline of the Chicago, North Shore, and Milwaukee Railroad from the time of the original request for abandonment, first considered by the Interstate Commerce Commission in 1949, to the eventual approval of this request in 1955, nearly six years later (Hilton and Due, 1964: 336). Complete closure of the electric railway occurred only after extensive court battles. While the initial request of May 1958 was approved by the ICC in November 1959, it was not until January 1, 1963 that the courts finally allowed closure.

The foregoing discussion, of course, must be placed in context. In most organizations, especially firms, owners retain the right to determine the organization's future, and the decision to continue a nonperforming organization as often as not reflects noneconomic considerations of prestige or power. However, ownership prerogatives are not absolute and have eroded in recent years. Just as the courts have increasingly held that long-term employees have property rights in their jobs and therefore cannot be dismissed at will, the public has begun to view closings or relocations of large organizations as public rather than private concerns. This is reflected in statutes requiring early notification of intended plant closings, in occasional suits brought against employers planning massive layoffs, and in government bailouts (and in some instances, temporary takeovers) of failing private firms. Even absent these legal and governmental constraints, however, powerful social constraints inhibit the willingness of owners to close marginal operations. The theoretical models sketched here are intended to illustrate the nature of these social constraints.

Extending the Model

The model of permanent failure sketched applies mainly to firms, for which the distinction between owners and dependent actors can be drawn relatively easily. An important question is whether this model can be extended to other kinds of organizations generally, and specifically to nonprofit and government agencies for which there are no owners and no financial profits to be realized. We believe that the model can be extended directly in the case of government or nonprofit monopolies and with surprising results when service organizations encounter competition. We shall also argue that an important insight arises from extending the model to nonprofits and government, namely that the elements of permanent failure exist in the nonprofit and public sectors but are combined in somewhat different ways than in private firms.

Owners versus dependent actors.   We begin this section by asking whether the distinction between owners and dependent actors or any similar distinction is meaningful outside profit enterprises. We believe that it is, provided that we keep in mind that motivations in nonbusiness settings may be quite complicated.[15]

In public administration, the difference between policy making and policy implementation is widely understood. Policy makers confront choices between programs and may, like owners, move their resources elsewhere. Policy makers are also motivated by long-term payoffs, particularly continuation in office. Public agencies charged with program implementation face policy choices with much less equanimity than do policymakers as their own continuation may be at stake, and the beneficiaries of programs often have no alternatives to existing programs and are therefore highly dependent.

In the nonprofit sector, the distinction between persons in ownerlike roles, whom we shall call sponsors, and dependents is somewhat more complicated. Nonprofits are generally formed for broad charitable, educational, or service purposes. Sponsors are normally committed to these purposes (and hence to maintaining nonprofit organizations). Like owners of family firms, sponsors are rarely motivated to move their commitments elsewhere—although they can sometimes move their commitments to new programs within an existing organization. At the same time, the constituencies of nonprofits may be *very* dependent upon these organizations, indeed literally "locked in" in some instances (one need think only of those nonhospitalized retarded persons who rely entirely upon nonprofit organizations for their housing and care). To the extent that dependent actors have few alternatives, as is the case here and in declining industry contexts in the private sector, they will be strongly committed to maintaining the organization. The commonly observed response to low performance under monopoly conditions is attempted reform of an existing organization.

There are, of course, instances in which sponsors are more attached to existing organizations than clients or customers (e.g., small performing arts organizations in large metropolitan areas). Organizations of this type, like family businesses, do not fit the permanent failure framework to the extent that maintenance rests on the desire of sponsors to maximize prestige.

In general, then, the distinction between actors in ownership or equivalent roles (e.g., policy makers, sponsors) and dependent actors can hold for all kinds of organizations, provided that the distinction is understood as more analytic than literal. Owners or their equivalents normally have the power to shift resources or commitments and are motivated to do so by considerations of profit or other indexes of overall performance, as problematic as the latter may be (see Kanter and Summers, 1987). Managers' motivation is more problematic in the public nonprofit sector, except when objectives are clearly defined. Sometimes managers have greater dependence on public organizations than their clients have.[16] Under monopoly conditions, clients may have strong motivation to seek higher performance rather than exit, giving rise to reform attempts. But under conditions of competition, clients may move from low-performing to high-performing organizations, leaving managers uniquely in a position of dependence.

Dependence and power.   There is no reason to believe that the relationship of dependence to power differs across firms, public agencies, and not-for-profit organizations. Other things being equal, the greater the dependence, the greater the motivation to exercise power (although as noted earlier, the array of interests and actions determines the form of power exercised). There is, however, reason to believe that the dependencies surrounding public agencies and nonprofit organizations may sometimes be greater than the dependencies surrounding firms. Public agencies and nonprofits may be natural monopolists whereas firms usually are not; moreover, the services provided by the public and nonprofit sectors may be more vital than for-profit services. Partly for this reason, the relationship of power to performance is more problematic (and therefore theoretically interesting) for public and nonprofit organizations than it is for firms.

There are, of course, conditions under which actors normally considered to be dependent seek to discontinue an organization, acting against the preferences of managers or sponsors seeking to maintain it despite manifestly low performance. These conditions obtain when choices are available for clients of nonprofit and government organizations: If alternatives for service exist, clients tend to choose the higher performing organization. The summing of these individual choices produces massive effects on survival probabilities for these organizations. In one recent study of hospitals from 1959 to 1979, the effects of providing alternative sources of service were dramatically evident. When legal change created a set of alternatives for indigent and low-income persons, allowing them to contract for health services at a wide range of hospitals rather than simply at the county hospital, the effects were swift and powerful: County hospitals closed at a much higher rate, while other hospitals that provided higher quality service were more protected from closure (Zucker, 1987c).

Power and performance.   At this point, our central theoretical propositions bear repeating. Organizations can be understood as containing diverse interests, which coincide under conditions of high performance. Low performance, however, triggers cleavages: Actors in ownership or equivalent roles in most cases seek fundamental changes, while dependent actors in most cases seek continuation of existing organizational patterns. In this model, to the extent that dependent actors acquire effective power, changes may be blocked, and initial low performance is transformed into sustained low performance or permanent failure.

A question we must now confront concerns whether initial low performance is transformed into permanent failure outside the realm of for-profit organizations. Let us consider the matter of performance first. Clearly, public and nonprofit organizations are more prone to pursue multiple and contradictory objectives than are firms. How numerous and how inconsistent these objectives are is open to question. Certain forces, however, will tend toward fewer and more consistent performance measures, while other forces will have the opposite effect. Generally, performance will be defined narrowly to the extent that (a) elites dominate an organization, (b) a high degree of professionalization exists, and (c) the organization performs a technical function, outputs of which are measurable. Performance will be construed much more broadly, by contrast, to the extent that (a) the norm of participative democratic governance operates, (b) the interests of multiple constituencies are given recognition, sometimes in the formal structure or rules of an organization, and (c) the organization's function is nontechnical and outputs elude measurement.

Two conclusions can be drawn immediately from these observations about performance. First, performance can be construed quite narrowly in certain public and nonprofit settings. For example, the operations of a city's water and sewage treatment facilities are usually assessed on technical (if not efficiency) grounds; to a slightly lesser extent, the same holds for fire and police services. Second, even when broad definitions of performance exist, operative performance criteria tend to be much more specific. Abstract ends give way to concrete means and operational programs of behavior as one moves from higher to lower levels of administration (Simon, 1947; March and Simon, 1958). This process is most dramatic in government, for which overall goals are always elusive yet major subunits, which are specialized by purpose, often have rather specific operating objectives. The impact of internal differentiation on the specificity of objectives has not been studied as extensively in nonprofit organizations as in government, but there is no reason to believe that nonprofits differ significantly from public agencies in this regard.

Let us now consider responses to low performance in public and nonprofit settings. Here too, internal specialization also plays a role. At the level of the entire organization, public agencies cannot abandon crucial functions, just as nonprofits cannot abandon broad value commitments. Schools, sanitation, and the national defense must be provided, regardless; the missions of nonprofits cannot be changed save with great difficulty (Sills, 1957). But choices do remain at lower levels of administration: public versus private refuse collection, basic medical research versus public health programs, aid to the homeless versus aid to employed but impoverished citizens. Each of these choices affects dependent actors, who are motivated to challenge the prerogatives of decision makers when their interests are threatened. And dependent actors do challenge the prerogatives of decision makers in public and nonprofit settings with some frequency. This may occur because of an ethos of openness and democratic governance, but there is an additional explanation for the contentiousness of government and some nonprofit organizations: Dependent actors can appeal to the ill-defined values and commitments of the larger organization when they are dissatisfied with its actions or the actions of one of its units. The same possibility does not exist for firms in which objectives are defined fairly narrowly even at the highest levels.

The essential similarity of firms with public and nonprofit organizations, then, is this: At some level, all organizations have fairly well-defined objectives. Low performance confronts owners, policy makers, sponsors, or their equivalents with choices as to how best to meet these objectives. Many alternatives are not in the interest of dependent actors who have substantial investments in established routines, causing dependent actors to resist change using whatever influence they can muster. An important difference between firms and public and nonprofit organizations lies in the kinds of values and commitments present at the highest levels. For firms, these values and commitments are likely to be somewhat well-defined and consistent. For public and nonprofit agencies, values and commitments are more ambiguous, encouraging dependent actors to exercise power and creating the possibility that dependent actors' grievances will, in fact, be heard.

Whether or not dependents' exercise of power constitutes failure or success under these circumstances is a matter of language. To the extent that their initiatives intended to augment performance are blocked, policy makers or sponsors will experience failure while dependent actors will perceive success, not only for themselves but also for the values of openness and democratic governance. Language aside, however, it appears that similar processes operate across organizations of different types. Low performance (from the perspective of owners or their equivalents) triggers divergences of interest that, in turn, block change. Initial low performance is thus transformed to sustained low performance, or permanent failure.

A revised motivational model.   Less commonly, though it is increasingly the case, clients of public and nonprofit organizations are confronted with choices: They can use the services of one agency or another, and can use whatever criteria they deem important to select the agency. In so doing, they alter the survival probabilities of the organizations in all but the most extreme cases. What is interesting here is that the selection is seldom based on price of service, since the dependent actors almost never pay for the service. Hence, efficiency criteria disappear from the performance equation and effectiveness criteria dominate. The services that are used are those of high quality, with indifference to price, and selection of organizations then rests on reputation for high quality rather than efficiency (see the discussion of evidence on this point in Zucker, 1987c).

Compare for a moment clients' motivation with the motivation of managers in the public sector. If managers are rewarded for performance at all, they are rewarded for delivery of low-cost services—an efficiency focused measure, not necessarily related to effectiveness. The recent drive for privatization of public services has been justified largely on efficiency grounds. Owing to competition, private firms are expected to deliver lower cost services than is the public sector.[17] Thus the one performance criterion of importance to clients—effectiveness—is of little significance to public sector managers.

Consider, now, the relationship of declining effectiveness (not efficiency) to clients' and managers' motivations to maintain existing public-sector organizations. Managers' favor organizational maintenance regardless, as they are neither rewarded for high performance nor deprived for low performance. Absent competition, clients will also favor maintaining the organization in face of declining effectiveness—but they will also want to change the organization. Given competition, however, clients' motivation to maintain organizations may well fall below managers' as effectiveness declines. Indeed, it is entirely possible that clients' motivation to maintain competing public organizations will decline as effectiveness deteriorates, just as owners' motivation to maintain low performing firms declines with deteriorating performance. The pattern sketched in Figure 5.1, then, is partly inverted for public organizations having competitors. Whereas in Figure 5.1, dependents favored organizational maintenance regardless, only managers favor organizational maintenance in this instance. And whereas in Figure 5.1, owners' motivation to continue organizations declined with performance, here clients' motivation declines with deteriorating effectiveness.

The model we present for public (and to some extent for nonprofit) organizations, then, is more complex than the one presented for private organizations. If monopoly conditions prevail, then the model developed in the private sector works well with minor modification—dependent actors favor organizational maintenance. If competition for service exists, the less common case, then clients who are normally regarded as dependent actors have both the motivation and the power (individual, not collective) to alter the survival probabilities of the organization. In general, survival probabilities of organizations delivering high quality services will improve regardless of cost; survival probabilities will decrease for organizations producing low quality outputs. Clients will be indifferent to the efficiency component of performance, however, since others pay the bill for the services provided.

But such selection for effective organizations is the exception rather than the rule. As we shall see in the next section, it can be difficult to terminate public organizations, even those with no remaining functions.

Permanent failure in extremis. We should consider, finally, instances in which public or nonprofit organizations continue even though they are bereft of clients. An organization's clientele may dwindle because its mission has been fulfilled or because its clients have gone elsewhere,[18] the latter caused sometimes, but not always, by abysmal performance. The question we wish to raise is whether sufficiently powerful dependent actors remain under these circumstances, and, if so, whether the nature of their power illustrates any special characteristics of permanent failure in public and nonprofit organizations.

Our impression, although we have no systematic data with which to confirm it, is that due process guarantees empower virtually any group that is dependent upon the continuation of a public-sector organization. A minor illustration is of interest: Immediately after voter approval of California's Proposition 13, the Los Angeles County supervisors attempted to close several county hospitals and health centers but were frustrated in this effort for two years. The opposition came not from patients but from Department of Health Services administrators and staff, who filed lawsuits alleging that the supervisors had not given the State of California the required 60 days' notice before closing a health facility (see *Los Angeles Times,* 1981a, 1981b, 1981c). Although these suits were eventually quashed or rendered moot, they sustained facilities whose patients had gone elsewhere and had no interest in their continuance.

A general proposition emerges from this discussion of permanent failure in public and nonprofit organizations, a proposition that applies with some force to for-profit firms. The proposition asserts that social constraints impede the operation of economic or economic-like forces that would sustain high performing organizations and shut low performers. Statutory restrictions on closures of plants and government facilities sustain low performance directly. Another constraint sustaining nonperforming organizations arises from the ambiguous and often contradictory missions of government and nonprofit organizations that often legitimate the grievances of dependent actors and thereby force reconsideration of decisions to terminate agencies with few palpable functions or outputs. Other constraints giving rise to permanent failure were suggested in Table 5.2 and the accompanying discussion. Full-scale community-based resource mobilization, revolutionary action, and the overt exercise of the power of dependents are not frequent events and are not asserted to be necessary conditions for sustained low performance in firms. But in subtle and very subdued forms these processes are ubiquitous, and they erode ownership prerogatives thereby contributing to permanent failure.

Notes

1. Moreover, a theory attempting to explain exogenous causes of low performance would be fraught with all of the difficulties of the studies of efficiency cited above.

2. The role of nonowners in the governance of organizations is by no means unique to our model. Williamson (1985: chap. 12), for example, considers explicitly how transaction-specific assets of groups such as workers, suppliers, and members of the larger community can be safeguarded by the participation of these groups in the firms's governance structure. Williamson argues that efficient transactions are sometimes achieved by representatives of the board of directors, sometimes by contractual provisions, sometimes by governmental regulation. No particular motivational assumptions are made other than that efficient solutions are preferred to inefficient ones. Here, motivational assumptions are exploited: Owners seek high performance (as measured by accomplishment of approved objectives), whereas dependent actors seek preservation of the organization.

3. A commonsense argument suggests that owners maintain nonperforming organizations in order to divert their assets for

personal use. This argument, we believe, underscores the importance of the permanent failure thesis: Not only is it the case that the bleeding of organizational assets runs contrary to official objectives, but the benefits of such diversion cannot be considered in negotiating a sale or salvage price. Owners holding such nontransferable assets, therefore, are also dependent on their organizations in the same way that workers', suppliers', and customers' ties to the firm are nontransferable.

4. This assumes, of course, the existence of an alternative strategy. Firms whose assets have zero salvage value have few alternatives save for closure; moreover, provided that no substantial losses are incurred, closure may not be attractive.

5. The same point is made, although not derived from systematic premises, by Kimberly et al. (1983) and Stinchcombe (1983, 1986).

6. This is somewhat in contrast to Hirschman (1970), who assumes monopolists to be lazy rather than exploitive of their environments.

7. One notable exception may be the wildcat strike; see the next discussion below and Gouldner (1954).

8. Springs Mills is described in Harvard Business School cases #92D685-063 and #9-685-0647/86. HBS Case Services, Harvard Business School, MA 02163.

9. Dependence is seldom complete; the two parties to the exchange are reciprocally dependent on each other, though one may have relatively more power and less dependence on the other. Means to gain power relative to the other, then, rest on the reciprocal quality.

10. Threatened withdrawal of services would not serve as a mechanism in plant closure since retention of workers is unnecessary. Even in the case of declining industries, threatened withdrawal is unlikely to have much impact, since earlier layoffs are likely to have provided a ready labor pool of those with unique assets that are critical to the firm's performance (in economist's terms, non-fungibility, idiosyncratic skills); nor would legitimation or conferring of status on the more powerful party, since owners and other claimants already exercise clearly legitimated power. Finally, finding alternative sources would only increase the likelihood of demise of the plant or the industry.

11. External resources have been discussed in the resource mobilization literature, but very few generalizations have emerged. See McCarthy and Zald (1977), Tilly (1978), Eisinger (1973).

12. Eisenstadt (1978) argues that revolution occurs when separate antistate movements, such as religious groups and elite divisions, simultaneously but independently seek overthrow of the status quo; most recently, Goldstone (1986) argues that the English Revolution had its origin in the convergence of multiple independent conflicts in the early 1600s, and Brustein (1987) points out that the French Revolution arose from the convergence of elite/state conflicts and peasant/landlord conflicts. Of course, in each of these studies an important precondition is that the state must have some internal conflict, with elite defection, weak economy, and so on. Skocpol (1979) argues convincingly that some kind of state breakdown precedes the revolution. We do not explicitly borrow this part of the argument, though it is clear that declining organizational performance plays a somewhat analogous, "activating" role.

13. We are indebted to George Hilton for suggesting this example.

14. This is very similar to the pluralistic conception of community politics: Issue-focused temporary coalitions form to influence political action.

15. Motivations in business settings may also be complicated, but simplifying assumptions, for example, owners seek profit, do not seem as awkward as in other settings. This awkwardness is illustrated by the motivational assumptions made in models of conduct in the public sector, for example, of bureaucrats as budget maximizers (Niskanen, 1971) or as maximizers of trust relations (Breton and Wintrobe, 1982).

16. For example, the number of health professionals in a county significantly decreases the likelihood of hospital closure and is also a strong predictor of new hospital foundings (Zucker, 1987c, forthcoming).

17. Evidence for hospitals indicates, once again, that third-party payment (in this case, private insurance) reduces dramatically the importance of efficiency. Concern with effectiveness dominates (Zucker, 1987c).

18. The bureau administering pensions to Garibaldi War widows (see note 1, Chapter 2, this volume) and the situation of Los Angeles parochial high schools illustrate this phenomenon.

6. Organizational Responses
to Permanent Failure

We now wish to examine organizational responses to permanent failure caused by the exercise of power on the part of dependents. We assume owners and/or managers to be aware of forces pressing for maintenance of low-performing units and to act to offset their impact. Cost-cutting measures, of course, are often taken to correct low performance: Such measures normally include contracting for goods and services that were once supplied internally, aggressive pursuit of concessions in labor contracts, and threatened if not actual relocation of plants and offices. But cost-cutting does little to augment the range of choices available to owners or residual claimants—indeed, it may constrain choices further—and it does little to limit the power of actors seeking the maintenance of existing organizations.

The argument to be made here is unusual but straightforward: Strategies of growth, innovation in organizational structure, privatization, and shifting employment relationships are pursued in order to augment the range of choices available to owners or their equivalents and, therefore, to limit the power of dependent actors. Growth, while commonly observed, is poorly explained in both the sociological and economic literatures on organizations. Changes in organizational structure are normally understood by sociologists to be outcomes of size, technology, and environmental contingencies (Scott, 1975), and by economists to be outcomes of efficiency constraints that compel minimization of transaction costs (Williamson, 1975). Privatization of nonprofit or public enterprises is normally understood by economists as a means of imposing market discipline and incentives and thereby enhancing productive efficiency (Borcherding, 1977). Change in the nature of employment relationships, recently observed by sociologists, are also understood, albeit implicitly, as having indirect as well as direct efficiency functions (Pfeffer and Baron, 1986). Here, we wish to propose that growth, innovations in organizational structures, privatization, and changes in employment relationships may be implemented for essentially political purposes, albeit purposes intended ultimately to restore high performance.

One further argument will be made: Should strategies of growth, organizational innovation, privatization, and externalization of employment be unavailable or should they have been exhausted, managers may intervene directly in order to confront the dilemmas posed by permanent failure. If the bounds of ordinary managerial authority are exceeded at this point, a combination of persuasion and force are used to build consensus about alternatives to permanent failure. Managerial intervention, like managerial strategies aimed at limiting the power of dependent actors, is thus understood as political action intended to restore satisfactory if not optimal performance.

Strategic Actions in Response to Power

We shall review first some strategies aimed at averting or reversing sustained low performance and then discuss how the doctrine of strategic management has altered the balance of power between owners or their equivalents and dependent actors in modern organizations.

Growth.   Consider first the aim of augmenting the choices available to owners or their equivalents. Choices can be augmented in two ways, by avoiding difficult zero-sum decisions in which one party's gain is another's loss, and by adding relatively inexperienced personnel who are more dependent upon their bosses than are veterans. Growth helps augment choices in both respects.[1] Decisions concerning the allocation of new resources generated by growth are much less constrained and contentious than are reallocation decisions. Moreover, growth shifts the demography of organizations by increasing the proportion of new members, who are less inclined than are veterans to resist management initiatives. As noted by Starbuck (1965: 474), "New members of an old organization . . . tend to be attracted by goals or task structure. They tend not to be attracted by the social structure." Even though growth may offer short-term relief from permanent failure, its long-run effect may be the opposite: Large size gives rise to internal differentiation in organizations (Blau and Schoenherr, 1971) and hence to multiple interests, some of which may diverge from interests of owners or their equivalents. For this reason, the strategy of growth alone may be insufficient to sustain attention to tasks and performance.

Organizational innovation. Consider next the aim of isolating and removing dependent actors from effective influence. One principal mechanism for isolating dependent actors is construction of organizational structures that separate strategic decisions, particularly choices as to whether or not to continue a business enterprise, from day-to-day operating decisions. Multiunit and conglomerate organizations have this property. A defining characteristic of multiunit and conglomerate forms of organization is separation of operational from strategic decisions—the former remaining in operating divisions, the latter removed to the central office. Multiunits and conglomerates, then, not only formalize strategic choice as an identifiable business activity, but in most instances they also separate strategic choices physically from more routine decisions.

The isolation of strategic from operational decisions is normally understood as having direct benefits for efficiency: Relentless assessment of performance by strategic planners is said to inhibit reciprocities, preferences for internal procurement, and tendencies toward uneconomic expansion (Williamson, 1975). Here, we wish to emphasize that separating strategic from operational decisions may shift the balance of power away from dependent actors. Stated simply, this separation places much greater distance between dependent groups, whether workers, suppliers, or customers, and the persons they wish to influence, owners and executives responsible for deciding whether to continue or discontinue individual business enterprises. Since dependent actors tend to cluster about operating units, not the central office, effective mobilization of power is rendered difficult once strategic decisions are removed from routine operations. To the extent that strategic decisions are removed from operating units, then, alignments of interest, coalitions, and collective action mobilizing dependent actors are rendered less effective.[2] Multiunit and conglomerate organizational structures may, therefore, limit the influence of dependent actors and in some instances be constructed specifically for this purpose.

Privatization.   The aim of removing dependent actors from effective influence can also be served by privatization of public-sector enterprises. Privatization is not an unambiguous concept (Starr, 1985), but it generally refers to removal of activities from direct administrative control of government and, often, substitution of contractual for organizational relationships. Privatization is often justified as offering efficiency advantages, and certain comparisons of public with private service delivery sustain this argument, particularly when comparisons involve routine services such as refuse collection and utilities (Savas, 1982). Privatization appears to offer fewer efficiency advantages, and in some instances disadvantages, in nonroutine services (Bendick, 1985).

We wish to propose that the efficiency advantages of privatization, to the extent that they exist, are secondary to its political advantages. Work conducted in the public sector is subject to a number of constraints that may be absent from private enterprise. The formal constraints include legislative oversight, civil service regulations, prevailing-wage clauses, virtually mandating union labor (and therefore union influence), appeal procedures for unfavorable decisions, a variety of mechanisms requiring timely notice of and citizen input into decisions of public bodies, and extensive postauditing of expenditures. Informal constraints affecting public enterprises include political patronage and a sense that the benefits (or spoils) of public organizations ought to be shared equally by constituent groups. Together, these formal and informal constraints render dependent actors extremely influential. Indeed, in some instances, legislative mandates place client groups in control of public agencies serving their needs (Meyer and Steinback, 1986).

Effectively, if not formally, privatization removes many of the constraints on public bodies, reducing dependents' influence. Removal of dependent actors from influence is often followed by increases in efficiency, reflecting, at least from an economic perspective, improved performance. But improved efficiency can occur through several routes. One is reduced operating costs—which are almost always claimed by advocates of privatization. Another route to improved performance, again from an economic perspective, is reduced services or increased fees, as appears to have occurred in medicine (Starr, 1982; Light, 1986). Thus while privatization may have the nearly certain effect of diminishing dependent actors' influence, its effect on costs are uncertain, depending on whether removal of dependents from influence leaves owners and managers free to reduce costs, enhance revenues, or both.

Externalization of employment.   A recent article asks whether employment is now being "'externalized" from organizations. Pfeffer and Baron (1986) note that much of organizational theory developed during the period when bureaucratic control was expanding, giving rise to the assumption that direct hierarchical control of workers would continue to grow. This assumption, they argue, is now suspect: Not only have the physical proximity of workers to employers and the duration of jobs decreased, but so have direct administrative controls over the work of employees. Several possible benefits of externalization are hypothesized, but most important for the present discussion is flexibility:

> Organizations require flexibility not only in terms of numbers of employees, but also in terms of the skills those employees possess. When new skills are required, one merely contracts with a different company or uses a different set of temporary workers . . . this is precisely why many organizations have externalized much of their data and word processing—they will not have to worry about making fixed investments in personnel and training, only to find the workforce made obsolete by new hardware and software [Pfeffer and Baron, 1986: 25].

We need only substitute "recalcitrant" for "obsolete" to understand externalization of labor as an organizational response to permanent failure. Short-term contract workers have no property rights to their jobs, and hence no effective means of resisting organizational changes intended to improve performance—again, performance from the perspective of ownership interests.

Table 6.1 portrays several organizational strategies in response to constraints upon choices available to owners and effective influence

TABLE 6.1
Organizational Response to Permanent Failure

| | Isolate Dependents | |
	(-)	(+)
(-) Augment Choices	- - -	divisionalization/ externalization
(+)	growth/ privatization	conglomeration/ inside contracting?

on the part of dependent actors. Should owners of firms seek augmentation of choices, a strategy of growth that increases alternatives may be implemented. Choices may also be augmented, for public agencies, through privatization. Should owners seek isolation of dependent actors from effective influence, the multiunit form of organization, which separates strategic from operating decisions, may be put in place. Dependent actors can also be isolated by externalizing employment. Should both augmented choices and diminished influence of dependent actors be sought, the conglomerate strategy, which normally yields both growth and removal of strategic choices from operating units, may be attempted. But choices can also be augmented and dependent actors' influence diminished by practices reminiscent of inside contracting, whereby employers (whether firms or public bodies) place themselves at arm's length from those who directly supervise work, and supervisors, in turn, seek workers in an unstructured and fully competitive labor market.

The notion that strategies of growth and reorganization along the lines of the multiunit and conglomerate forms may be pursued in response to constraints on choice and the power of dependent actors helps explain the preference for multiunit and conglomerate organizational forms in the face of evidence, noted previously, that organizational form has little impact on performance.[3] Over time, dependent actors acquire skills in acting collectively, limiting or preventing choices that offer improved performance but also risk the existence of an organization. And over time, in response, organizations pursue strategies intended to offset the power of dependent actors. Organizations evolve toward growth and the multiunit and conglomerate forms, therefore, partly in order to maintain the possibility of choices consistent with acceptable levels of performance, and partly to limit the influence of dependent actors upon these choices. But organizations may also evolve in a very different direction, toward more contractual or contractlike relationships and less hierarchical administration in response to the same conditions. Choices between simple and complex organizational forms as well as between internal labor markets and an externalized work force are driven by the imperatives of isolating dependent actors from influence and preserving the alternatives available to owners or their equivalents.[4]

Several implications arise from this account of organizational strategies in response to the power of dependent actors. To begin, the advantages of growth, separation of strategic from operational decisions that is characteristic of the multiunit and conglomerate forms, restriction of rights of access and appeal that occurs with privatization, and powerlessness associated with part-time contract work are essentially political. All may help relieve constraints that would otherwise limit choices severely. Because they allow owners and their agents greater latitude in making choices, enhanced performance is more likely, but so is outright failure. For this reason, superior efficiency does not necessarily inhere in large and complex organizational forms, just as efficiency does not necessarily inhere in private organizations or in organizations having mainly part-time and temporary workers. However, the correlation of performance to persistence is likely to be higher, hence the likelihood of permanent failure lower when choices are available to owners or their equivalents. Another implication is that the low reputation of government (Lipset and Schneider, 1983) may be more a function of constraints that limit choices than of governmental failures. Growth, organizational innovation, and changes in employment relations are much more easily decided in board rooms than in legislative chambers—if they can be considered at all in the public sector, and usually they cannot be. A major advantage of privatization may be simply that it opens alternatives that are otherwise unavailable, and thereby the possibility of either outright success or outright failure. A final implication is this: To the extent that specific mechanisms exist or are invented for the purpose of creating an identity of interests among actors associated with organizations, neither growth nor elaborate administrative structures may be required to preserve the capability of making fundamental choices. Japanese firms, for example, encourage consensus by training employees in organizational values (Pascale and Athos, 1981: 49-52); it may be for this reason that they also tend to involve more people in decisions while having taller hierarchies (Lincoln et al., 1986) than do their U.S. counterparts.

The doctrine of strategic management and the balance of power within organizations. The objectives of preserving or augmenting alternatives while limiting the power of dependent actors is justified in concepts of strategic management. Strategic management concepts assert that owners and managers have the right, indeed the obligation, to allocate capital resources to their most efficient uses.[5] These concepts form the cornerstone of much financial as well as organizational theory. Indeed, they are so widely accepted that it is difficult to conceive of their absence nowadays. Yet an alternative is conceivable: It is the notion that organizations should do what they do efficiently rather than change what they do in order to reap greater profits. The idea that firms or organizations—in contrast to individual financiers or "robber barons"—are free to move capital to whatever uses they deem fit is a relatively recent development. Throughout much of the nineteenth century, corporate charters were not freely granted; when incorporation did occur, it was for specific purposes.[6] Even after restrictions on incorporation eased, businesses tended to concentrate their activities in a single industry. Only in the last 30 years have individual firms spanned multiple industries, directing capital to different uses depending upon their expected return; only in the last 15 years have management texts added strategic choice to the list of basic management functions.

The conventional argument for mobility of capital is economic: Large firms substitute internal for external capital markets owing to the efficiencies of the former. We wish to suggest a somewhat different explanation, namely that concepts of strategic management open choices that were previously unavailable to owners or residual claimants and simultaneously delegitimate claims made by actors who are dependent upon organizations. When corporate activities are restricted, owners of a nonperforming business can choose only to continue or discontinue the enterprise. Given these alternatives, the arguments for continuance made by and on behalf of dependent actors may be overwhelming given that discontinuance promises little or no return for all parties involved. Given strategic management concepts, however, the assets of a nonperforming business can legitimately be diverted into enterprises promising a higher rate of return, offsetting to a great extent the arguments for continuance and sometimes making moot these arguments altogether once an existing business has been stripped of resources. Strategic management concepts, thus, help circumvent the power of actors who value organization more than performance.

The intersection of motivations and risks among owners or residual claimants and among actors dependent on organizations, the power of dependent actors, and organizational responses to power suggests a model explaining why the combination of high persistence and low performance—permanent failure—occurs with some frequency. The first element in the model is low performance, which gives rise in turn to divergent interest among owners and dependent actors: The former seek high performance, the latter preservation of organization. While changes intended to improve performance may be essentially costless to owners of nonperforming firms, they may prove very costly to dependent actors whose livelihoods are potentially jeopardized. These divergent interests give rise to the third element in the model, mobilization of dependent actors through alignment of interests, coalition, and collective action. Such mobilization seeks to block changes inimical to the interests of dependent actors. Organizational responses appear over time, sometimes in growth strategies, sometimes in organizational structures removing strategic choices from operating units in which dependent actors are clustered and most easily mobilized, sometimes in privatization, sometimes in externalization of workers, sometimes in different combinations of these. One might imagine that further mobilization of dependent actors occurs, particularly as organizational responses to power create new dependencies with the passage of time. The causal relations among divergent interests, collective action seeking to limit owners' prerogatives, and organizational responses are described in Figure 6.1. Whether or not these organizational responses aimed at isolating and atomizing dependent actors succeed in offsetting forces tending toward organizational maintenance has not been ascertained in research. What is important is that Figure 6.1 offers a causal explanation for high persistence, low performance organizations, and for managerial strategies in response to sustained low performance.

Permanent Failure and the
Role of Management

The idea of permanently failing organizations bears some implications for thinking about management and, indeed, may require reconsideration of some established notions. Traditionally, management has been thought of as having certain functions or responsibilities that contribute directly to the overall effectiveness and efficiency of the organization. These functions include planning, organizing, directing, and the like (Gulick and Urwick, 1937), maintaining communication and cooperation (Barnard, 1939), and shaping decision premises that permit subordinates to make complicated decisions within bounded rationality limits (Simon, 1947). More recently, the functions imputed to management have shifted somewhat: The unique contributions of managers are thought to be communication (Mintzberg, 1973) and skill in directing organizations toward fundamental values and objectives while maintaining simultan-

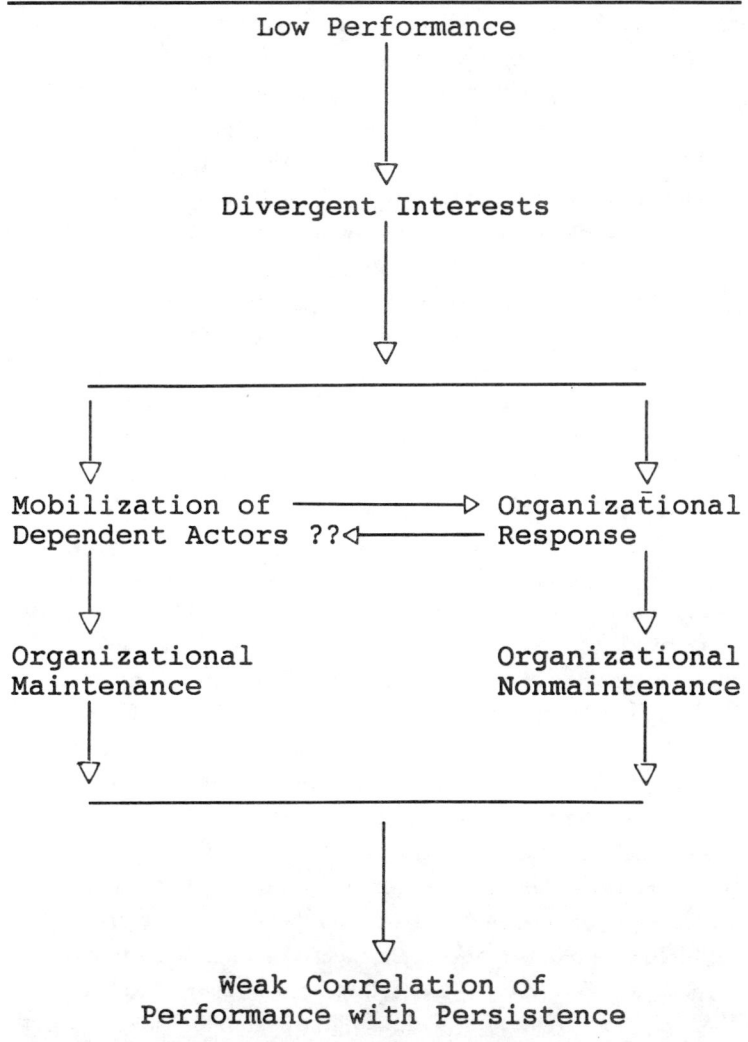

Figure 6.1   The Weak Correlation of Performance with Persistence

eously "loose" and "tight" properties (Peters and Waterman, 1982). The functions served by management have never been the subject of careful empirical research. Whereas myriad studies have explored, albeit inconclusively, the impact of different leadership traits on organizations (Stodgill, 1974), virtually no attention has been directed toward identifying vital managerial actions or activities absent which long-term viability or performance of the organization is threatened.

This anomaly is reflected in economic writings on organizations. From a strictly evolutionary perspective, management is of little consequence for organizations. Efficient organizations survive; inefficient organizations do not and are displaced by more efficient forms. To be sure, behavioral routines as well as search and selection processes may influence evolutionary processes (Nelson and Winter, 1982), but uniquely managerial contributions to routines, search, and selection are not specified. Even when management is treated explicitly as contributing to outcomes, the nature of its contribution remains opaque. For example, formal models construing organizations as production functions and management as one of several factors of production do not specify with any precision how managers contribute to outcomes (Breton and Wintrobe, 1982: 23). Management is instead a "black box," the content of which is never made explicit.

Aside from the failure of theory to specify in any rigorous manner the functions of management, several other facts are of interest. One fact is the displacement of entrepreneurial by managerial leadership relatively early in many firms' history—at least for firms that survive infancy.[7] Another is the growth of management. As already noted, ratios of administrative to production and of supervisory to nonsupervisory personnel have mushroomed in the last 30 years (Meyer et al., 1985: chap. 2), although their growth has moderated recently (Meyer, 1987). Finally, conflict among managerial personnel is more typical than atypical of larger organizations. Case studies (e.g., Dalton, 1959; Crozier, 1964) reveal ongoing struggles for power in both business and bureaucratic settings. Power and contests for control are treated as outcomes of uncertainty or imbalances in resources, consistent with the theories reviewed earlier. Pfeffer's (1982) analysis extends this earlier work by tracing some consequences of power in organizational settings, specifically legitimation and institutionalization of power as authority relations. Neither Pfeffer nor anyone else, however, has dealt simultaneously with the problems of why managerial has displaced entrepreneurial leadership, why the functions of managers are so poorly specified in organizational theory, why the ranks of management have swollen so rapidly, and why conflict is endemic in managerial roles.

A partial resolution of this problem, we argue, requires that our normal presuppositions about organizations be revised, perhaps reversed. As outlined at the beginning of this monograph, there is a tendency to think of organizations as efficient rather than as inefficient, as performing rather than as nonperforming. As the reader knows well by now, we are skeptical of models assuming efficiency. Our skepticism about efficiency models now takes on an added dimension. Not only are efficiency models incapable of explaining the combination of high persistence yet low performance in organizations, but they also cannot explain parsimoniously the actions of managers, and the growth and contentiousness surrounding many managerial tasks. To be sure, efficiency models can claim, *ex post facto,* that managerial actions, growth, and fractiousness (and for that matter, anything else) have positive consequences for efficiency. But this logic defeats the very proposition that organizations are efficient: Were organizations normally and naturally high performers, the same management characteristics hypothesized to maintain efficiency would not be needed. A different set of state-of-the-world assumptions, departing significantly from the efficiency model, may be needed to account for the salient characteristics of management.

We wish to suggest that the role of management, particularly in established organizations, is best understood within the framework of permanent failure. Organizations tend toward permanent failure, it will be recalled, because low performance that arises from exogenous conditions causes interests to diverge and contests for power to develop subsequently. While all parties may agree that sustained low performance is an unsatisfactory state of affairs, they may disagree strongly as to the desirability of alternative paths from permanent failure. (This disagreement and the paths from permanent failure were portrayed in Figure 5.2.) A task of management, perhaps its principal task, is to reclaim control of the organization, often by negotiating among various interest groups in and around the organization so that alternatives to permanent failure are rendered viable. This task is ill-defined. Were disparate interests commensurable, that is, were simple incentives capable of aligning diverse interests, the problem of permanent failure would not arise. This task is also complex. As interests increase, the difficulty of negotiating among them multiplies geometrically. And the task is conflict-ridden. Even when the continuation of an enterprise or portion of an enterprise is not at stake, choices aimed at averting permanent failure carry consequences for peoples' livelihoods and lives.

The uncertain, complicated, and conflict-ridden character of managerial tasks under conditions of permanent failure appear in somewhat exaggerated form when dramatic actions are required to prevent outright failure of an organization, but the contrast is mainly a matter of degree. Lee Iacocca's (1985) account of his stewardship of the Chrysler Corporation provides a rare description of how diverse interest groups were persuaded to act, sometimes cooperatively but sometimes not, in order to save his firm. In retrospect, the public arguments made by Iacocca seem unusual and possibly internally inconsistent as well as inconsistent with his subsequent actions. On the one hand, a philosophy of free enterprise and, by implication, self-reliance was espoused. On the other hand, government regulation and exorbitant union wages were blamed for Chrysler's high costs, the former justifying government intervention. At the same time, Iacocca called attention to externalities associated with a possible Chrysler bankruptcy, particularly unemployment and associated welfare costs. Together, these arguments produced government loan guarantees and wage concessions on the part of the unions, preserving Chrysler. But the Chrysler Corporation became profitable only after massive layoffs and further cost-cutting measures were instituted, yielding some of the same outcomes, at least in the short run, that the bailout was intended to avert.

Two elements should be emphasized here. First, Iacocca's actions, while carefully calculated, were not wholly rational. They were neither derived from first principles nor entirely consistent with one another. They were instead tactical measures. Slightly different circumstances might have demanded dramatically different arguments and actions. Thus action that is nonrational in this sense may be fundamental to the role of management in large organizations. Second, the imminence of outright failure (the upper rightmost cell in Figure 5.2), or what appeared to be its imminence, rendered actions that were risky and that subsequently proved costly to dependent workers and suppliers more acceptable than they would have been under conditions of permanent failure. Thus the power of management increases as organizations move toward outright failure. Management power is weakest, therefore, when outright failure cannot occur, as in essential public services and regulated industries under conditions of low competition.[8]

A full account of the role of management is not possible in the context of this monograph. Our intent is merely to suggest that the concept of permanent failure, the idea that organizations tend toward sustained low performance under certain circumstances, provides a theoretical basis for thinking about managerial tasks, a basis not otherwise available in the organizational literature. This way of thinking about management does not yield simple or deterministic propositions about managerial behavior. But it improves upon previous thinking, which offers mainly functional explanations for the evolution from entrepreneurial to managerial leadership in many firms by accounting for certain observable features of managerial tasks, particularly their proliferation and their uncertain and conflict-ridden character.

Permanent Failure and Public Administration

The reader might ask, and reasonably so, whether permanent failure is not endemic in public administration, whether the constraints on public sector managers preclude effective responses to low performance. The research and theory reviewed in the previous chapters apply mainly to private-sector organizations, yet the overall argument seems to fit public organizations as well or better. After all, is it not the public sector rather than the private that is stereotyped as conflicted and incapable of decisions? And is it not the public sector rather than the private that stands accused of wasteful and inefficient conduct, which is not readily corrected?

The theory of permanent failure, it will be remembered, assumes the possibility of high performance, albeit a possibility that is not always realized. And the theory distinguishes initial low performance from sustained low performance: Initial low performance owing to exogenous causes triggers divisions of interest between owners and dependent actors that, in turn, prevent or delay decisions aimed at restoring high performance. As stated, the theory assumes some conditions present in private firms that cannot be taken for granted in public organizations. These include official objectives (such as profit) that are reasonably well understood, performance measures capturing these objectives more or less reliably, the correspondence of interests among actors in and around organizations so long as performance is high, and conflicting interests once performance deteriorates.

The public sector is different. As often as not, public-sector objectives are ill-defined and interests in and around public organizations are divergent from the outset. Public organizations, therefore, carry from their beginnings many of the liabilities that emerge only much later, if at all, in private firms. The liabilities of public organizations are outlined vividly in Jerry Mashaw's book, *Bureaucratic Justice* (1983), which describes the complicated and, in many respects, inconsistent official objectives of the Social Security Title II (Disability Insurance) and Title XVI (Supplemental Security Income). Consider first the problem of determining eligibility for disability benefits.

> The congressional choice with respect to who is to be supported by the disability program is apparently absolute. Persons are disabled if *unable* to work by reason of their *medical condition* at any job in the *national* economy. But on closer examination, the underlying incoherence of the disability standard reveals the legislature's distress at its choice. A basic policy question for the legislature, for example, was whether the disability program should support (a) persons who have medical problems and

cannot find work on that account or (b) only persons who have medical problems and on that account are neither substantially gainfully employed nor indeed able to work. The Congress explicitly chose the latter standard of disability.

This definition of disability is rather peculiar, but peculiar for a clear reason. Congress has attempted to separate disability from unemployment. The latter risk has its own separately structured insurance program.

As SSA pursues [its] administrative task it must surely wonder what rigid adherence to the statutory definition might mean. The statutory standard suggests that the answer to both the question, "Would the claimant ever be hired?" and the question "Is the claimant disabled?" should be, "No." It presumes that ability to do a job has some meaning divorced from its operative economic context. But can it really be sensible to say that although a person is, because of medical impairments, too far back in the labor queue ever to be employed, yet the same person is not disabled because of these same medical impairments" [Mashaw, 1983: 52-53]?

Somewhat differently, a person must be not merely unemployed but also unemployable in order to be classified as disabled.

While the distinction between unemployed (and therefore ineligible for benefits) and unemployable (and therefore eligible) is sensible in theory, it is surrounded by myriad difficulties in practice. The difficulties arise from several sources. One is the reluctance of the Congress to maintain an absolute distinction between the merely unemployed and the disabled. To illustrate: Age is considered in determining disability, since, as Mashaw points out, Congress wished disability insurance to serve partly as an early retirement benefit for those too young for ordinary Social Security benefits but excluded from the work force owing to the combination of age and medical problems. Similarly, education and prior work experience are also considered in disability determination, reflecting Congress's concern for the plight of the poorly educated and chronically unemployed. Compassion for the elderly and disadvantaged, in other words, has complicated the objectives of the Disability Income program.

The distinction between unemployed and unemployable is further clouded by competing bureaucratic, professional, and legal values in the system for administering and adjudicating disability insurance claims. To illustrate: While medical evidence is considered in determining whether or not an applicant for DI benefits is in fact disabled, the *opinions* of physicians and other professionals are explicitly excluded from consideration. Detailed categorical regulations are instead used to determine disability, but these, in turn, pose myriad problems of interpretation. The regulations state, for example, that arthritis with abduction of both arms at 90 degrees is grounds for medical disability. But Mashaw (1983) asks:

> Is abduction of one arm at 130° and the other at 50° the equivalent of both at 90°? Would any combination less than 180° suffice? Or is some less mechanical and more "functional" approach to capacity intended? But if so, what is the function by which equivalence is measured [p. 112]?

Tension between bureaucratic and legal values also pervades the determination of disability. During the 1970s, some 1.25 million claims for Social Security disability benefits were filed annually; of those claims denied, roughly 250,000 were appealed at the state agency level for reconsideration, and denials of these appeals resulted in about 150,000 requests for hearings before administrative law judges. On average, 15% of appeals at the state level reversed initial decisions to deny benefits, whereas 50% of appeals taken before administrative law judges—employees of Social Security, but governed by the federal Administrative Procedures Act rather than the Social Security statutes—were granted. The high reversal rate at the administrative law judge level caused the Social Security Administration to implement a "Quality Assurance Program," whereby judges deviating significantly from the 50% reversal rate were counseled and admonished to bring their decisions in line with national averages. Within a single organization, then, bureaucratic exigencies, principally budget restrictions that work against applicants, and judicial independence, which often affords applicants the benefit of the doubt, are on a collision course.[9]

Mashaw suggests that these competing objectives are not readily reconciled for two reasons. First, as should now be clear, the DI program's different objectives are inherently irreconcilable. Second, it is simply not in the interest of the Social Security apparatus to attempt rationalization of them. Inevitably, overt conflict, now suppressed by the ambiguity of the system, would accompany any attempt to impose rigid controls on decisions with the result that SSA would "be unable to present itself as all things to all interests, and those in the Congress and the affected populations who perceive threats to their interests will strike back" (Mashaw, 1983: 69). Bureaucratic rationality along the lines of the Weberian model, therefore, is severely limited; in Mashaw's words, "a compromised and sometimes uncontrollable system" (p. 75) is the result of a "complex and compromised reality" (p. 78).

Two questions about the theory of permanently failing organizations are raised by this account of the Social Security Disability Insurance program. First, and most pointed, can we speak of the DI program as permanently failing? Our answer, like the definition of disability, is somewhat equivocal, but ultimately it is closer to no than yes. Two related reasons cause us to hesitate before labeling the disability program as a failure. First, as Mashaw points out, it is difficult to imagine how the present disability insurance program could have been made more rational and therefore efficient without offending key constituencies. Vague and inconsistent procedures and objectives were deliberately built into the DI program from the outset because no feasible alternative existed. Second, given inconsistent premises and the elusiveness of efficiency or performance measures, the model of permanent failure sketched here—the progression from high performance to initial low performance to sustained low performance—describes the experience of the DI system poorly. To be sure, like permanently failing firms, the Social Security Disability program is fraught with conflict and indecision. But unlike permanently failing firms, there exists no ideal and, most important, no experience of success or high performance with which to compare actual achievements.

The case of Social Security Disability Insurance Program is not unique. Ill-defined objectives and divergent interests are built deliberately into many public programs, rendering performance measures elusive and conflict and indecision endemic. To call these agencies permanent failures and therefore to search for more efficient private-sector alternatives sweeps beneath the table the larger question of why efficiency is expected of the public sector, or, better, why the public bureaucracy is disparaged as a model of inefficient administration. The answer, we believe, lies in the peculiar history of the United States, where the rhetoric of "businesslike" administration has spilled over from the private sector into the public, and indeed shaped the public sector indelibly during the reform era (Meyer et al., 1985: chap. 1), creating unrealistic expectations of the latter. The reality of public administration, of course, has frequently fallen short of this ideal, owing more to the nature of its tasks than to ineptitude or malfeasance.

A final question, then, concerns whether or not the experience of the public sector renders permanent failure is too strong an indictment of private firms that never perform for their owners but nonetheless linger on. We wish to offer two observations. On the one hand, organizations providing jobs for employees and goods and services for customers without profiting their shareholders are certainly not outright failures even if they fail the test of financial performance. Our theory, in fact, suggests that such organizations are often maintained. On the other hand, the idea of permanent failure is a useful corrective to ideas of economists and others anticipating that such organizations cannot, indeed should not, survive.

Notes

1. Of course, if firm performance is extremely low, growth may not be a possible strategy.

2. It is not surprising, therefore, that plant closures follow swiftly in the aftermath of conglomerate mergers. See Stern et al. (1979: chap. 2). In general, it may be easier to terminate subunits, as long as such termination doesn't threaten the existence of the whole.

3. Innovations in organizational form improve performance of the initial adopters. Hoping that success will generalize, other

organizations adopt without independent analysis (Armour and Teece, 1978; Tolbert and Zucker, 1983).

4. The structural changes reduce dependent actors' influence at the center, while under some conditions actually giving dependent actors more control over decisions in the local exit.

5. Needless to say, efficiency is in respect to owners' or their equivalents' interests, not other actors'.

6. Bellah et. al. (1985: 289) note, additionally, that corporate charters were granted only upon demonstration that the public good would be served by incorporation.

7. The case of Apple Computer illustrates displacement of entrepreneurial by managerial leadership styles. See Harvard Business School Case on "John Sculley at Apple Computer," #9-486-001, 6/83. HBS Case Services, Harvard Business School, Boston, MA 02163. Under Apple's early leadership, the firm was fraught with "a lot of gun slinging and little target practice. If you make a mistake, somehow it's buried in the growth of the company. The politically savvy people move on and somebody else gets nailed for it" (see foregoing case, p. 5). When John Sculley succeeded Mike Markkula as president and CEO of Apple, he focused on an innovative product strategy, but he also made some procedural changes: Memos were limited to a single page, phone messages were to be answered promptly, formal meetings were established to review and correct mistakes, and open voting and democratic decision making, the consequence of which was that no project was overruled, were eliminated.

8. Lipsky (1980) attributes the power of "street-level bureaucrats," such as police, welfare workers, and teachers, to the discretion inherent in their jobs. Our interpretation is somewhat different: Discretion is exercised because management is powerless given the essential nature of street-level bureaucrats' jobs. That their jobs are indispensable is indicated by Lipsky's data showing few if any cutbacks in street-level bureaucrat positions during the urban fiscal crisis of the late 1970s.

9. Conflicts between judicial and executive branches of government are commonplace (see, for example, *Los Angeles Times,* 1987). What is distinctive about the Social Security Administration is its effort to regulate, through quotas, judicial decisions.

7. Permanent Failure and the Sociology of Organizations

The idea of permanent failure is central to the sociology of organizations. If high persistence, low performance organizations exist in substantial numbers, which we believe to be the case, and if the causes of simultaneous high persistence and low performance lie in the diverse interests that accumulate over time in and around organizations, then the maintenance of low performing organizations must be understood as natural and normal outcomes of social processes. Most important, these processes operate as much within organizations—for example, in interactions between dependent employees seeking to maintain employment and managers seeking to shift firms' investments—as between organizations and their environments.

The theory of permanent failure therefore directs inquiry to the connection between the formation of organizations and their subsequent maintenance. This connection between internal processes and organizational maintenance is largely overlooked in theories of environmental determination, in which wholly exogenousforces are assumed to govern the structure and existence of organizations. The connection is also overlooked in conventional economic thinking in which the only admissible question asks how formal organization contributes to efficiency outcomes. A sociology of organizations, we argue, must transcend the limits of both environmental determination and utility maximization by asking how ongoing patterns of interaction among actors located within and around organizations sustain existing organizational patterns, environmental and economic constraints aside.

Structure and Process in the Sociology of Organizations

In its initial stages, sociological research on organizations was directed toward understanding the relationship of structure to organizational process—patterns of interaction within organizations. The classic case studies—Blau's *The Dynamics of Bureaucracy* (1955), Gouldner's *Patterns of Industrial Bureaucracy* (1954), and

Selznick's *TVA and the Grass Roots* (1949)—drew upon Weber's (1946) bureaucratic model, but in doing so they identified unanticipated and, in some respects, dysfunctional aspects of organizations.

The core proposition of these studies might be stated as follows: Organizational process defeats, to some extent, the purposes for which organizations were created in the first place. Michel Crozier's *The Bureaucratic Phenomenon* (1964) carried this line of argument to its limit in proposing that the key elements of the bureaucratic model contribute to a "vicious circle" of dysfunctions culminating in organizational stasis or total incapacity for change. Indeed, Crozier defined bureaucracy as organization unable to correct its own errors. He did not consider the possibility that large organizations become, for a variety of reasons, more stable over time and hence have progressively less incentive to correct their errors.

Over the past two decades, sociological research on organizations has retreated steadily from this initial concern with the consequences of internal structure for organizational process. The causes of this retreat were both substantive and methodological. Substantively, the focus on dysfunctions may have been too narrow to sustain further studies of organizational structure and process. Methodologically, studies of dysfunctional patterns were confined to single organizations and therefore, at least on statistical grounds, of uncertain generality.

The retreat from process, and especially from *rational* process occurred in two stages. In the first stage, research covering multiple organizations displaced case studies, and interrelations among characteristics describing the formal authority structures of organizations were sought. Process was ignored: Taxonomies of organizational structures were developed initially (Aston studies) and were followed by causal models in which structural measures served as both independent and dependent variables (Blau and Schoenherr, 1971). The theoretical justification for research focusing solely on structural attributes of organizations was never fully established, however.[1] It may be that for this reason actual results of research on organizational structures were sometimes disappointing. Pervasive effects of size were found: Larger organizations were more differentiated than smaller ones. But the effects of other crucial variables, such as technology, were either nonlinear or inconsistent. (See review articles by Scott, 1975 and Kimberly, 1976, as well as Blau and Meyer, 1987: chap. 5.)

The second stage of the retreat from organizational process was marked by the idea that environments determine organizations. As noted in Chapter 2, even though several distinct theories of environmental determination emerged, all of these theories viewed organizations as shaped more by external than by internal forces. The results of research testing theories of environmental determination were, as noted earlier, sometimes disappointing, as organizations were in many instances resilient in the face of external pressures. Even so, concepts of environmental determination shifted thinking about organizations rather dramatically, for they moved the locus of causality from within to without organizations.

The notion of environmental determination was appealing on several grounds, two in particular. Environmental determination was derived from a conceptual model of organizations of high generality, the open-systems model. The behavior of organizations was thus expected to parallel that of other systems, biotic systems in particular. Environmental determination also settled—or appeared to settle—issues of causality that had plagued studies of organizational structure. Whereas structural theory did not specify whether, for example, size precedes technology or technology precedes size, the theory of environmental determination unambiguously gave primacy to external forces.[2]

Theories of environmental determination did not ignore process, but they overlooked processes within organizations, focusing instead on other formal organizations as significant actors. Implicitly, patterns of interaction between organizations and their environments—or, more specifically, interaction between actors in organizations and their counterparts located in other organizations—were assumed to be of greater significance than interaction within organizations. This assumption contradicted much of earlier theory, which treated organizations as decision-making systems limiting the stimuli and therefore the alternatives available to individual persons. And it was rendered suspect by subsequent research results, which showed, in many instances, that peoples' perceptions of environments depend more on organizational characteristics than upon objectively determined properties of environments (the pertinent literature is reviewed in Meyer, 1987).

Ultimately, theories of environmental determination are unable to deal satisfactorily with the question of why organizations exist. If environments construct, shape, and destroy organizations absent significant resistances, then it is not clear why organizations are needed at all. Under such conditions, organizations *qua* organizations add no significant independent effects. Environmental determination should operate as effectively on individual persons as on organizations, rendering the latter little more than emergent and labile patterns of interaction shaped by larger forces. Let us put this somewhat differently: On logical grounds alone, it is impossible to derive organizational inertia from environmental change. If, on the other hand, organizations offer significant resistances to environmental forces, then the nature and effects of these resistances should be discovered. We have argued that these resistances are rooted in processes in and around organizations, specifically stalemates arising when the interests of diverse constituencies, some of which are only loosely organized, are brought into conflict. Notably, language that describes these resistances does not explain these resistances. To speak, for example, of certain organizations as "institutionalized" or "inertial," hence somewhat shielded from immediate environmental pressures, begs the question rather than answers it.

Permanent Failure and Organizational Process

Despite mainstream organizational theory's flight from organizational processes, discussions of process have not disappeared entirely from the field. The connection of structure to process is salient in two literatures, organizational demography, and transaction-cost economics.[3]

Little need be said about the first—organizational demography—save to repeat its central premise: Opportunities for individual people in organizations (i.e., internal processes allocating people to jobs) are determined by the structure of organizations. Organizational demography has developed in several directions, including studies tracing the impact of organizational hierarchies on flows of individual persons through various positions in organizations (White, 1970; Stewman and Konda, 1983), studies examining the effects of work force composition (e.g., average seniority, proportion female) on advancement and earnings attainment (Pfeffer, 1983; Pfeffer and Davis-Blake, 1987; Lawrence, 1987) and studies examining the effects of demography on other internal organizational processes, notably interaction (Kanter, 1977). These studies have focused on affects of organizations on individual people, and they have not been concerned with performance and persistence outcomes central to this monograph.

Transaction-cost economics, although differing totally in substance from organizational demography, also retains, in principle, a focus on process.[4] Oliver Williamson's (1975) organizational failures framework finds efficiency advantages in certain organizational processes, including the emergence of common languages or codes, the development of convergent expectations, and internal policing or auditing of conduct.[5] All of these, Williamson argues, help overcome bounded rationality limits and opportunistic inclinations that impede efficiency, hence they contribute to preference for organizational as opposed to market coordination of activity. Williamson's claims for efficiency advantages of organizations over nonorganizational modes of coordination have been challenged. Granovetter (1985), in particular, notes that imputing unobserved efficiency advantages to extant structures returns us to a form of functionalism long discarded from sociology. This may or may not be the case: Williamson (1987) dissents vehemently. Unarguably, however, Williamson's claim that organizational processes within organizations enhances efficiency and Granovetter's rejoinder that the same processes may impair efficiency have reintroduced thinking about process into mainstream organizational theory.

The theory of permanent failure extends this discussion of organizational process in two ways. First, the theory of permanent failure derives propositions about behavior from assumptions about motivations of actors in and around organizations. It asserts that actors value both performance and organization—generally, owners or their equivalents value performance and dependent actors organization, though under conditions of competition in public sector/service delivery, these relations reverse—and argues that some tension will exist between these motivations. The theory of permanent failure argues further that these motivations are not aligned easily, especially when external conditions cause performance to decline in the private sector. Initial low performance galvanizes the motivation to maintain organizations into action, limiting the choices available to owners and their agents. Second, the theory of permanent failure focuses simultaneously on performance and persistence outcomes rather than solely on one or the other, as has heretofore been the case. Because it hypothesizes certain conditions in organizations that favor high persistence and high performance and other conditions that favor high persistence yet low performance, the theory does not contain the functionalist bias that finds positive performance consequences for almost all observed features of organizations. At the same time, the theory does not reason by counterexample: It offers causal propositions anticipating where sustained low performance is to be expected and where it is not. And the theory raises the question, previously ignored, of whether the same causes give rise to stability and continuity in organizations and, at the same time, low performance.

Economists have challenged sociologists to offer nonadventitious explanations of organizations that do not, in one way or another, rely upon efficiency principles. The theory of permanent failure offers an alternative to efficiency models of organizations, and in particular to models asserting that organizations maximize net benefits accruing to owners or residual claimants. To be sure, the theory admits that actors in and around organizations pursue their own interests. Indeed, it relies rather heavily on this assumption. But the theory of permanent failure argues that this pursuit of self-interest cannot always be limited by incentives or control mechanisms, particularly when low performance renders incentives scarce and control through the usual inducements—salary, advancement, career prospects— weak to nonexistent.[6] A dynamic process leading to sustained low performance is thus envisaged. The theory of permanent failure is therefore nonadventitious in that it is derived from evidence showing performance and persistence to have different time paths and different concomitants, yet it does not rely upon efficiency principles to explain the enduring features of organizations.

Permanent Failure and Organizational Research

In this penultimate section, we explore the implications of permanent failure for research on organizations. A substantial agenda is at hand. On the one hand, the idea of permanent failure suggests that the relation of performance to persistence in organizations is problematic, requiring research that explores this relationship. This research is macroscopic, as entire organizations are the most appropriate units of analysis. On the other hand, divisions of interest among individuals and subgroups within organizations are hypothesized to give rise to permanent failure. Pursuing this hypothesis requires research of a more microscopic nature, as subgroups rather than entire organizations are the natural units of analysis.

Macroscopic research: identifying sustained low performance. In Chapter 3, we reviewed the pertinent literature on persistence and performance. What studies exist suggest the relation of the two to be uncertain and, in all likelihood, weak. But there are few such studies, and none were designed specifically to test the impact of performance constraints compared to other constraints affecting the survival of organizations.

Several technical difficulties obtain when one seeks to pursue the relation of organizational performance to persistence. One, noted earlier, is the measurement of performance: The greater the range of organizations encompassed by performance measures, the weaker their associations with one another. A further difficulty lies in the dynamic nature of persistence. The foregoing discussion proceeded as if static comparisons of organizational performance and persistence were possible. They are not. Although most (but not all) performance measures are static, organizational persistence or longevity is inherently a dynamic attribute—it is the likelihood of survival to the next time interval. Static measures alone, therefore, cannot identify permanently failing organizations. Instead, the unique characteristic of permanently failing organizations is *sustained* low performance: Permanent failure is marked by lengthy intervals of low performance. In most cases, we believe, this low performance is a permanent condition, but these intervals may be terminated by a return to high performance in some cases—or they may also end in organizational death. Alternatively, sustained low performance may be terminated by a redefinition of performance standards.[7]

Macroscopic research focusing on entire organizations has the task of determining whether or not there is a prima facie case for permanent failure. Macroscopic research must determine whether sustained low performance occurs commonly or is infrequent and, if the former, whether intervals of low performance are balanced by periods of high performance or are endemic to certain kinds of organizations—for example, regulated industries or monopolies. Given the theory outlined here, macroscopic research cannot identify the ultimate causes of permanent failure, although it can identify its concomitants. More microscopic inquiries are needed to determine the sources of sustained low performance.

Microscopic research: the causes of sustained low performance.   We have argued that the causes of permanent failure, sustained low performance, lie as much within as without organizations and, in particular, in the inability of organizations to make choices yielding either outright failure or success. In the private sector, choices are blocked, as outlined in Chapter 4, when dependent actors acquire power that is normally reserved to owners, residual claimants, or their equivalents in organizations. Competition in the public or nonprofit sector also empowers dependent actors, but with far different consequences: Clients seek to preserve high performing organizations, while managers are aligned with other dependent actors, including employees, in attempting to maintain the organization, regardless of performance. Microscopic research is needed to capture the processes leading to empowerment of dependent actors. Of particular interest is the hypothesis that power accrues to dependent actors as their interests converge or their capacity for joint action develops. Microscopic research is also needed to gauge organizational responses to the power of dependent actors. Ultimately, microscopic and macroscopic research must be joined in order to test fully the theory of permanent failure. To the extent that the theory has a central proposition, it is this: As power accrues to dependent actors in organizations, performance deteriorates while persistence is enhanced. Less precisely but more poignantly, politics degrades performance but enhances persistence in organizations. Both microscopic data on processes affecting dependent actors' power and macroscopic data on performance and persistence are needed to test this proposition fully. Thus not only will a test of the theory of permanent failure require data describing a large number of organizations, but this test will also require rather detailed information about internal processes of each.

Summary and Afterword

This monograph outlined a theory of permanently failing organizations, organizations characterized by high persistence yet low performance. In the past, theories of organizations, whether originating in sociology or economics, have assumed severe performance constraints on organizations. Some recent theories have relaxed these performance constraints, but have substituted for them notions of environmental determination, whereby organizations that fit external demands are at an advantage over those that do not fit. This monograph moves a step further (some might say ahead, others behind) by removing environmental constraints somewhat from organizations. Organizations are composed of actors, some of whom are more sensitized than others to external forces demanding performance. Under conditions of satisfactory or better than satisfactory performance, the interests of actors valuing performance and those with other priorities, which we labeled organization, are easily aligned, and ordinary economic incentives encourage performance maximization. When performance deteriorates, however, the alignment of interests is not easily maintained, decision making is blocked, and permanent failure, sustained low performance, results. Managerial intervention is needed to rescue organizations in the private sector from permanent failure; theories of organizational strategy can be understood as prescriptions for averting or correcting this pattern of sustained low performance.

Our theory is summarized in the following propositions:

I. Definition of permanent failure: the combination of low performance and high persistence in organizations, organizational maintenance under conditions of low performance, sustained low performance in organizations.

II. Propositions about permanent failure drawn from organizational theory:
   A. Permanent failure decreases to the extent that
      1. organizations seek efficiency or high performance and
      2. efficient high-performing organizations survive.
   B. Permanent failure increases to the extent that
      1. differentiated environments pose multiple constraints for organizations, only some of which are related to performance and
      2. organizations exercise power over environments.

III. Observations about permanent failure drawn from organizational research:
   A. Observations concerning the measurement of performance: performance measures are varied and weakly correlated with one another.
   B. Observations concerning concomitants of performance:
      1. While owner control often gives way to managerial control with age, the performance of owner-controlled

firms is sometimes superior to manager-controlled firms.

2. Although there is a tendency for firms to evolve from unitary to multiunit structures, there is little evidence showing organizational innovation to yield sustained improvements in performance.

3. Performance does not increase with organizational age; mature manager-controlled firms may perform poorly.

C. Observations concerning concomitants of persistence:

1. Organizations tend to evolve from specialist to generalist forms and from simple to complex organizational structures, generalist organizations and organizations with complex structures have, under some conditions, greater persistence than others, though subunits may have less persistence than others.

2. For firms, although not for public bureaus, organizational persistence increases with age.

D. Observations concerning the relationship of organizational performance to persistence:

1. Performance and persistence appear *not* to have similar causes.

2. Organizations protected by entry barriers or expecting high future returns, organizations in declining industries, and organizations pursuing multiple goals, such as family firms, persist for long intervals despite low performance.

IV. Propositions comprising a theory of permanent failure:

A. Motivations to maintain organizations must be distinguished from the power to do so.

1. So long as owners or their equivalents are motivated to maintain organizations, they will use their power to do so (generally, owners or their equivalents have the power to maintain or to terminate organizations);

2. So long as dependent actors (workers, suppliers, customers, the larger community) are motivated to maintain organizations, they will also use their power to do so (however, dependent actors do not normally have the power to maintain or terminate organizations).

B. Motivations to maintain organizations may converge or diverge, depending on performance.
   1. Under conditions of high performance, owners (or their equivalents) and dependent actors are motivated to maintain organizations (the interests of owners or their equivalents) and of dependent actors therefore converge.
   2. Under conditions of low performance, however, owners (or their equivalents) in the private sector are motivated to alter or terminate existing organizations, whereas dependent actors are motivated to maintain existing organizations. The interests of owners (or their equivalents) and of dependent actors therefore diverge.
      a. Under conditions of low performance in firms, owners (or their equivalents) favor action potentially restoring high performance but risking outright failure.
      b. Under conditions of low performance, dependent actors oppose action risking outright failure.
   3. Under conditions of low performance, owners (or, more commonly) managers in the public or nonprofit sector are *not* motivated to alter or terminate existing organizations. Motivation decreases linearly as ambiguity of objectives increases; when monopoly conditions exist, dependent actors (clients) will be interested primarily in maintaining organizations, though they may also be motivated to reform them; under competitive conditions, clients will select high effectiveness organizations, disregarding efficiency, selecting for quality and not cost; under competitive conditions, then, the interests of managers and clients diverge.
      a. Under conditions of low performance in public and nonprofit organizations, managers favor action potentially restoring high performance *only* when goals and objectives are relatively unambiguous.
      b. Under conditions of low performance in nonprofit or public organizations, clients will oppose action failure in a monopoly solution, but for such actions (if it is targeted on effectiveness, not efficiency) in a competitive situation.

   C. Dependent actors' motivation to maintain organizations under conditions of low performance may or may not be transformed into effective power to do so.

      1. Dependent actors, acting as individuals, have little power to maintain organizations.

      2. Joint action on the part of dependent actors, convergence of interests among them, or both can transform motivations to maintain organizations into effective power to maintain organizations.

         a. Joint action creates opposition to initiatives of owners (or their equivalents).

         b. Convergence of interests triggers redefinition of the prerogatives of owners (or their equivalents).

         c. Joint action and convergence of interests gives rise to communitywide mobilization in opposition to owners (or their equivalents).

   D. When dependent actors' motivation to maintain organizations is transformed into effective power, initial low performance evolves into sustained low performance, or permanent failure.

 V. Propositions concerning organizational responses to the power of dependent actors:

   A. Owners (or their equivalents) seek to augment their range of choices through strategies of

      1. growth

      2. externalization of employment.

   B. Owners (or their equivalents) seek to isolate dependent actors from effective influence through strategies of

      1. divisioning

      2. privatizing (public-sector organizations).

   C. The doctrine of strategic management facilitates organizational responses to permanent failure.

VI. Propositions derived from the theory of permanent failure:

   A. The likelihood of permanent failure increases as the number of dependent actors in and around organizations increases and as dependent actors are more readily mobilized; therefore

      1. above a threshold, large size gives rise to permanent failure

     2. dense ties among dependent actors give rise to permanent failure

     3. organizational age gives rise to permanent failure.

B. The likelihood of permanent failure increases as mechanisms enhancing dependent actors' influence are put into place; therefore

     1. permanent failure is more frequent in worker-managed than other firms

     2. permanent failure is more frequent in governmental than in other (whether profit or nonprofit) organizations.

C. The likelihood of permanent failure increases as alternatives available to dependent actors decrease; therefore

     1. the smaller the community, the greater the likelihood of permanent failure

     2. the weaker the national economy, the greater the likelihood of permanent failure.

D. The likelihood of permanent failure decreases, and, correspondingly, the likelihood of *either* success *or* outright failure increases as owners (or their equivalents) implement strategies aimed at averting sustained low performance. Therefore:

     1. cross sectional correlations between managerial strategies and performance outcomes will therefore be weak.

     2. over time, organizations implementing strategies aimed at averting or reversing permanent failure will displace others, provided that these responses do not trigger further mobilization of dependent actors.

E. The natural and normal condition of many organizations is permanent failure—sustained low performance—rather than high performance of success. Therefore:

     1. a principal function of management is averting or reversing patterns of permanent failure.

     2. over time, as forces tending toward permanent failure accumulate, innovative and entrepreneurial leadership styles give way to managerial leadership.

     3. over time, as forces tending toward permanent failure accumulate, managerial tasks and the uncertainty and conflict surrounding them increase.

The theory of permanent failure thus spans a wide range of organization-theoretic issues. Permanent failure is evident in processes of inertia and institutionalization noted by organizational researchers, in public-private differences observed by economists, and in the dilemmas of managerial choice discussed by students of organizational strategy. Consistent with the theory of permanent failure, the normal and natural state of organizations may be low performance rather than high performance, and all the more so as organizations grow in size and in complexity. Because organizations tend toward low performance, they demand constant attention and adjustment. Thus the theory of permanent failure not only accounts for the otherwise disparate observations about organizations that have emerged from several decades of research, but it may also account for the development of research and thinking intended to inform and improve our understanding of organizations.

Notes

1. To illustrate: While the initial intent of the studies undertaken by the Blau group was to provide an empirical basis for Weber's theory of bureaucracy (Blau, 1963), the principal theoretical contribution of these studies was a set of propositions about structural differentiation in organizations (Blau, 1970), which were quite different from Weber's ideas.

2. Not all approaches are equally deterministic. In several important works, it is suggested that organizations may choose their environments or at least influence and shape them (Pfeffer and Salancik, 1978; Child, 1977). These ideas are difficult to test empirically.

3. It goes almost without saying that the field of organizational strategy, given its concern with choices made by organizations and their consequences, also emphasizes process. But the field of strategy, unlike organizational demography and transaction-cost economics, is largely bereft of theory and therefore is not considered in this

section. As noted here the idea of permanent failure may provide a theoretical framework for studies of strategy.

4. The empirical literature surrounding transaction-cost economics has not, however, retained a focus on process, pursuing instead the causes (particularly in asset specificity) and efficiency consequences of different organizational forms.

5. But note that at least some of these same processes appear in markets. See Hirsch (1985) on the development of the language of corporate takeovers; see also the large literature on regulation concerning external policing and auditing of conduct.

6. As discussed in the previous chapter, under some conditions, structure can be used to limit the ability of subordinates to pursue their own self-interest. But generally, these strategies are limited to the largest organizations.

7. The literature on succession of goals is especially pertinent (see Sills, 1957).

References

Aiken, Michael and R. R. Alford (1970) "Community structure and innovation: the case of public housing." American Political Science Review 64: 843-864.

Alchian, Armen A. (1950) "Uncertainty, evolution, and economic theory." Journal of Political Economy 58: 214-223.

Alchian, Armen A. and Harold Demsetz (1972) "Production, information costs, and economic organization." American Economic Review 62: 777-795.

Alcorn, Pat B. (1982) Success and Survival in the Family-Owned Business. New York: McGraw-Hill.

Armour, H. O. and D. J. Teece (1978) "Organization structure and economic performance: a test of the multidivisional hypothesis." Bell Journal of Economics 9: 106-122.

Barnard, Chester (1939) The Functions of the Executive. Cambridge, MA: Harvard University Press.

Barnes, L. B. and S. A. Hershon (1976) "Transferring power in the family business." Harvard Business Review 54: 105-114.

Barnett, William P. and Glenn R. Carroll (1987) "Competition and mutualism among early telephone companies." Administrative Science Quarterly 32:400-421.

Barry, B. (1975) "The development of organization structure in the family firm." Journal of General Management 3: 42-60.

Bass, Frank M., Philippe Cattin, and Dick R. Wittink (1978) "Firm effects and industry effects in the analysis of market structure and profitability." Journal of Marketing Research 15: 3-10.

Baumol, William J. et al. (1970) "Earnings retention, new capital and the growth of the firm." Review of Economic Statistics 52: 345-355.

Baumol, William J., John C. Panzar, and Robert D. Willig (1982) Contestable Markets and the Theory of Industry Structure. New York: Harcourt Brace Jovanovich.

Beckhard, R. and W. G. Dyer, Jr. (1983) "Managing continuity in the family owned business." Organizational Dynamics (Summer): 5-12.

Bellah, Robert N., Richard Madsen, William M. Sullivan, Ann Swidler, and Steven M. Tipton (1985) Habits of the Heart. Berkeley: University of California Press.

Bendick, Marc (1985) Privatizing the Delivery of Social Welfare Services. Washington: Economic Policy Institute.

Ben-Prath, Y. (1980) "The F connection: families, friends, and firms in the organization of exchange." Population and Development Review 6 (1): 1-30.

Bernstein, P. (1980) Workplace Democratization. New Brunswick, NJ: Transaction.

Blau, Judith (1984) Architects and Firms. Cambridge: MIT Press.

Blau, Peter M. (1955) The Dynamics of Bureaucracy. Chicago: University of Chicago Press.

Blau, Peter M. (1963) "Critical remarks on Weber's theory of authority." American Political Science Review 57: 305-316.

Blau, Peter M. (1970) "A formal theory of differentiation in organizations." American Sociological Review 35: 201-218.

Blau, Peter M. and Marshall W. Meyer (1987) Bureaucracy and Modern Society (3rd ed.). New York: Random House.

Blau, Peter M. and Richard Schoenherr (1971) The Structure of Organizations. New York: Basic Books.

Blau, Peter M. and W. Richard Scott (1962) Formal Organizations. San Francisco: Chandler.

Borcherding, Thomas E. [ed.] (1977) Budgets and Bureaucrats: The Sources of Government Growth. Durham, NC: Duke University Press.

Boyle, Stanley E. (1970) "Pre-merger growth and profit characteristics of large conglomerate mergers in the United States: 1948-1968." St. Johns Law Review 44: 152-170.

Breton A. and R. Wintrobe (1982) The Logic of Bureaucratic Conduct. New York, Cambridge: Cambridge University Press.

Brustein, William (1987) "Political representation in France." Contemporary Sociology 16: 339.

Burns, Arthur F. (1934) Production Trends in the U.S. Since 1870. New York: National Bureau of Economic Research.

Burton, Richard M. and Borge Obel (1980) "A computer simulation test of the M-form hypothesis." Administrative Science Quarterly: 457-466.

Business Week (1987) "General Motors: what went wrong." March 16: 102-110.

Calder, G. H. (1961) "The peculiar problems of a family business." Business Horizons (Fall): 93-102.

Carroll, Glenn R. (1984a) "Organizational ecology," pp. 71-93 in Ralph H. Turner and James F. Short (eds.) Annual Review of Sociology. Palo Alto, CA: Annual Reviews.

Carroll, Glenn R. (1984b) Publish and Perish: A Dynamic Analysis of Organizational Mortality in the Newspaper Industries of Argentina, Ireland and the United States. Greenwich, CT: JAI.

Carroll, Glenn R. and J. Delacroix (1982) "Organizational mortality in the newspaper industries of Argentina and Ireland: an ecological approach." Administrative Science Quarterly 27: 169-198.

Carroll, Glenn R. and Paul Huo (1986) "Organizational task and institutional environments in ecological perspective: findings from the local newspaper industry." American Journal of Sociology 91: 838-873.

Casstevens, Thomas W. (1980) "Birth and death processes of government bureaus in the United States." Behavioral Science 25: 161-165.

Caves, Richard E. (1980) "Industrial organization, corporate strategy and structure." Journal of Economic Literature 18: 64-92.

Caves, Richard E. (1984) "Economic analysis and the quest for competitive advantage." American Economic Review 74: 127-132.

Caves, Richard E. and Michael Porter (1977) "From entry barriers to mobility barriers: conjectural decisions and contrived deterrence to new competition." Quarterly Journal of Economics 91: 241-261.

Caves, Richard E., Michael E. Porter, and Michael Spence (1980) Competition in the Open Economy: A Model Applied to Canada. Cambridge, MA: Harvard University Press.

Child, J. (1974) "Managerial and organizational factors associated with company performance—Part I." Journal of Management Studies 11: 175-189.

Child, J. (1975) "Managerial and organizational factors associated with company performance—Part II." Journal of Management Studies 12: 12-27.

Child, J. (1977) "Organizational design and performance: contingency theory and beyond." Organization and Administrative Science 8: 169-183.

Clark, Burton R. (1983) The Higher Educational System. Berkeley: University of California Press.

Clarkson, Kenneth W. (1972) "Some implications of property rights in hospital management." Journal of Law and Economics 40: 363-384.

Coleman, James S. (1974) Power and the Structure of Society. New York: Norton.

Cosyns, J. and R. Loveridge (1981) "The role of leadership in the genesis of producer cooperatives." Presented at the International Conference on Producer Cooperatives, Gilleleje, Denmark.

Crozier, Michel (1964) The Bureaucratic Phenomenon. Chicago: University of Chicago Press.

Crum, William Leonard (1939) Corporate Size and Earning Power. Cambridge, MA: Harvard University Press.

Cunningham, J. Barton (1977) "Approaches to the evaluation of organizational effectiveness." Academy of Management Review: 463-474.

Cyert, Richard (1978) "The management of universities of constant or decreasing size." Public Administration Review 38: 344-39.

Dalton, D. R., W. D. Todor, M. J. Spendolini, G. J. Fielding, and L. W. Porter (1980) "Organization structure and performance: a critical review." Academy of Management Review 5: 49-64.

Dalton, Melville (1959) Men Who Manage. New York: John Wiley.

Danco, L. A. (1982) Inside the Family Business. Englewood Cliffs, NJ: Prentice-Hall.

Davis, P. and D. Stern (1980) "Adaptation, survival and growth of the family business: an integrated systems perspective." Human Relations 34: 207-234.

Demsetz, Harold (1973) "Industry structure, market rivalry, and public policy." Journal of Law and Economics 12: 1-22.

DiMaggio, Paul J. and Walter W. Powell (1983) "The iron cage revisited: institutional isomorphism and collective rationality in organizational fields." American Sociological Review 48: 147-160.

Dowling, J. and J. Pfeffer (1975) "Organizational legitimacy." Pacific Sociological Review 18: 122-136.

Downs, Anthony (1967) Inside Bureaucracy. Boston: Little, Brown.

Due, John (1977) "Factors affecting the abandonment and survival of Class II railroads." Transportation Journal 14: 5-17.

Eisenstadt, S. N. (1978) Revolution and the Transformation of Societies: A Comparative Study of Civilizations. New York: Free Press.

Eisinger, Peter K. (1973) "Conditions of protest in American cities." American Political Science Review 67: 11-28.

Emerson, Robert M. (1962) "Power-dependence relations." American Sociological Review 27: 31-41.

Emerson, Robert M. (1964) "Power-dependence relations: two experiments." Sociometry 27: 282-298.

Etzioni, Amatai (1975) A Comparative Analysis of Complex Organizations (rev. ed.). New York: Free Press.

Fabricant, Solomon (1960) "Study of the size and efficiency of the American economy," pp. 52ff in E.A.G. Robinson (ed.) Economic Consequences of the Size of Nations. New York: St. Martin's.

Fama, Eugene F. (1980) "Agency problems and the theory of the firm." Journal of Political Economy 88: 288-307.

Fama, Eugene and Michael E. Jensen (1983a) "Separation of ownership and control." Journal of Law and Economics 26: 301-326.

Fama, Eugene and Michael E. Jensen (1983b) "Agency problems and residual claims." Journal of Law and Economics 26: 327-349.

Fisher, Franklin M. (1984) "The misuse of accounting rates of return: a reply." American Economic Review 74: 509-517.

Fisher, Franklin M. and John J. McGowan (1983) "On the misuse of accounting rates of return to infer monopoly profits." American Economic Review 73: 82-92.

Fisher, Lawrence and James Hirsch Lorie (1977) A Half-Century of Returns on Stocks and Bonds: Rates of Return on Investments in Common Stocks and on U.S. Treasury Securities 1926-1976. Chicago: University of Chicago Graduate School of Business.

Fizaine, Francoise (1968) "Analyse statistique de la croissance des entreprises selon l'age et la taille." Revue d'Economie Politique 78: 606-620.

Fligstein, Neil (1985) "The spread of the multidivisional form among large firms, 1919-1979." American Sociological Review 50: 377-391.

Freeman, John and Jack W. Brittain (1977) "Union merger process and industrial environment." Industrial Relations 2: 173-185.

Freeman, John, Glenn R. Carroll, and Michael T. Hannan (1983) "The liability of newness: age dependence in organizational death rates." American Sociological Review 48: 692-710.

Freeman, John H. and Michael T. Hannan (1983) "Niche width and the dynamics of organizational populations." American Journal of Sociology 88: 1116-1145.

Geiger, Roger L. (1980) Private Sectors in Education: Structure, Function, and Change in Eight Countries. New York: Free Press.

Glassman, Cynthia A. and Stephen A. Rhodes (1980) "Owner vs. manager control effects on bank performance." Review of Economics and Statistics 62: 263-270.

Gold, Bela (1964) "Industry growth patterns: theory and empirical results." Journal of Industrial Economics 13: 53-73.

Goldstone, Jack A. (1986) "State breakdown in the English Revolution." American Journal of Sociology 92: 257-322.

Goodgame, D. (1987) "Citizen McCabe." California Business (September): 46-53.

Gouldner, Alvin W. (1954) Patterns of Industrial Bureaucracy. Glencoe, IL: Free Press.

Gouldner, Alvin W. (1954) Wildcat Strike. Yellow Springs, Ohio: Antioch Press.

Granovetter, Mark (1985) "Economic action and social structure: the problem of embeddedness." American Journal of Sociology 91: 481-510.

Gulick, Luther and L. Urwick (1937) Papers on the Science of Administration. New York: Institute of Public Administration.

Hall, Marshall and Leonard Weiss (1967) "Firm size and profitability." Review of Economics and Statistics 49: 319-331.

Hammer, Tova H. and Robert N. Stern (1980) "Employee ownership: implications for the organizational distribution of power." Academy of Management Journal 23: 78-101.

Hannan, Michael T. and John H. Freeman (1977) "The population ecology of organizations." American Journal of Sociology 82: 929-964.

Hannan, Michael T. and John H. Freeman (1984) "Structural inertia and organizational change." American Sociological Review 49: 149-164.

Hatten, Kenneth J. and Dan E. Schendel (1977) "Heterogeneity within an industry: firm conduct in the U.S. brewing industry, 1952-71." Journal of Industrial Economics 26: 87-113.

Hatten, Kenneth J., Dan E. Schendel, and Arnold C. Cooper (1978) "A strategic model of the U.S. brewing industry, 1952-71." Academy of Management Journal 21: 592-610.

Hilton, George W. and John F. Due (1964) The Electric Interurban Railways in America. Stanford, CA: Stanford University Press.

Hirsch, Paul M. (1986) "From ambushes to golden parachutes: corporate takeovers as an instance of cultural framing and institutional integration." American Journal of Sociology 91: 800-837.

Hirschman, Albert O. (1970) Exit, Voice and Loyalty. Cambridge, MA: Harvard University Press.

Hochner, Arthur and Cherlyn Skromme Granrose (1985) "Sources and motivation to choose employee ownership as an alternative to job loss." Academy of Management Journal 28: 860-875.

Iacocca, Lee (1984) Iacocca. New York: Bantam.

James, David R. and Michael Soref (1981) "Profit constraints on managerial autonomy: managerial theory and the unmaking of the corporation president." Administrative Science Quarterly 46: 1-18.

Jensen, Michael E. and William Meckling (1976) "Theory of the firm: managerial behavior, agency costs, and ownership structure." Journal of Financial Economics 3: 305-360.

Kamerschen, David R. (1968) "The influence of ownership and control on profit rates." American Economic Review 58: 432-447.

Kanter, Rosabeth Moss (1977) Men and Women of the Corporation. New York: Basic Books.

Kanter, Rosabeth Moss and David V. Summers (1987) "Doing well while doing good: dilemmas of performance measurement in nonprofit organizations and the need for a multiple-constituency approach." Chapter 9 in The Nonprofit Sector: A Research Handbook, edited by Woody Powell. New Haven: Yale University Press.

Kaufman, Herbert (1976) Are Government Organizations Immortal? Washington, DC: Brookings Institution.

Kepner, Elaine (1983) "The family and the firm: a coevolutionary perspective." Organizational Dynamics (Summer): 57-70.

Kimberly, John R., Frederick Norling, and Janet A. Weiss (1983) "Pondering the performance puzzle," pp. 249-264 in Richard H. Hall and Robert E. Quinn (eds.) Organizational Theory and Public Policy. Beverly Hills, CA: Sage.

Kimberly, John (1976) "Organizational size and the structuralist perspective: a review, critique and proposal." Administrative Science Quarterly 21: 571-597.

Lansberg, I. (1983) "Managing human resources in family firms: the problem of institutional overlap." Organizational Dynamics (Summer): 39-46.

Larner, Robert J. (1970) Management Control and the Large Corporation. Cambridge, MA: Dunellen.

Lawrence, Barbara (1987) "An organizational theory of age effects," pp. 35-96 in Samuel Bacharach and Nancy D. Tomasso (eds.) Research in the Sociology of Organizations. Greenwich, CT: JAI.

Lawrence, Paul and Jay W. Lorsch (1967) Organization and Environment. Boston: Graduate School of Business Administration, Harvard University.

Lenz, R. T. (1981) "Determinants of organizational performance: an interdisciplinary review." Strategic Management Journal 2: 131-154.

Levinson, H. (1974) "How to make your family business more profitable." Journal of Small Business Management, October 12: (5): 35-41.

Light, Donald (1986) "Corporate medicine for profit." Scientific American 255 (December): 33-45.

Lincoln, James R., Mitsuyo Hanada, and Carey R. McBride (1986) "Organizational structure in Japanese and U.S. manufacturing." Administrative Science Quarterly 31: 338-364.

Lipset, Seymour Martin and William Schneider (1983) The Confidence Gap: Business, Labor and Government in the Public Mind. New York: Free Press.

Lipsky, Michael (1980) Street-Level Bureaucracy: Dilemmas of the Individual in Public Service. New York: Russell Sage.

Los Angeles Times (1981a) "State joins challenge to county health cuts." August 19: II-1, 8.

Los Angeles Times (1981b) "State official plans suit on health care." August 7: I-24.

Los Angeles Times (1981c) "Surplus won't help restore health cuts." September 1: II-1-2.

Los Angeles Times (1985) "'Now we can graduate'—teary-eyed Cathedral High Students exult." December 4: I-26.

Los Angeles Times (1987) "Court bars county closure of health clinics for poor." November 21: II-1.

Luhmann, Niklas (1982) "Ends, domination, and system: fundamental concepts and premises in the work of Max Weber," pp. 20-46 in The Differentiation of Society. New York: Columbia University Press.

Luhmann, Niklas (1985) "Authority in self-referencing systems." Address to the VI EGOS Colloquium, Stockholm, Sweden.

Macaulay, Stewart (1963) "Non-contractual relations in business: a preliminary study." American Sociological Review 28: 55-67.

March, James G. and Herbert A. Simon (with the collaboration of Harold Guetzkow) (1958) Organizations. New York: John Wiley.

Marcus, G. E. (1980) "Law in the development of dynastic families among American business elites: the domestication of capital and the capitalization of family." Law and Society Review 14: 859-903.

Marcus, Matityahu (1969) "Profitability and size of firm: some further evidence." Review of Economics and Statistics 51: 104-107.

Mashaw, Jerry (1983). Bureaucratic Justice. New Haven, CT: Yale University Press.

McCarthy, John D. and Mayer N. Zald (1977) "Resource mobilization and social movements: a partial theory." American Journal of Sociology 82: 1212-1241.

McConnell, Joseph L. (1945) "Corporate earnings by size of firm." Survey of Current Business 25.

McEachern, William A. (1975) Managerial Control and Performance. Lexington, MA: Lexington Books.

Mechanic, David (1962) "Sources of power of lower participants in complex organizations." Administrative Science Quarterly 7: 349-362.

Meeks, G. (1977) Disappointing Marriage: A Study of the Gains from Merger. Cambridge: Cambridge University Press.

Melicher, Ronald W. and David F. Rush (1974) "Evidence on the acquisition-related performance of conglomerate firms." Journal of Finance 7: 105-131.

Merton, Robert K. (1940) "Bureaucratic structure and personality." Social Forces 18: 560-568.

Metzgar, Jack (1980) "Plant shutdowns and worker response: the case of Johnstown, Pennsylvania." Socialist Review 53: 9-49.

Meyer, John W. and Brian Rowan (1977) "Institutionalized organizations: formal structure as myth and ceremony." American Journal of Sociology 83: 340-363.

Meyer, Marshall W. (1987) "The growth of public and private bureaucracies." Theory and Society.

Meyer, Marshall W. and Robin Steinback (1986) "Growth and complexity in services for the developmentally disabled: the case of California." Presented at the meetings of the American Sociological Association, New York.

Meyer, Marshall W., William Stevenson, and Stephen Webster (1985) Limits to Bureaucratic Growth. Berlin: de Gruyter.

Mintzberg, Henry (1973) The Nature of Managerial Work. New York: Harper & Row.

Monsen, R. Joseph, Jr. and Anthony Downs (1965) "A theory of large managerial firms." Journal of Political Economy 73: 221-236.

Monsen, R. Joseph, John S. Y. Chiu, and David E. Cooley (1968) "The effect of separation of ownership and control on the performance of the large firm." Quarterly Journal of Economics 82: 435-451.

Mueller, Dennis C. (1972) "A life cycle theory of the firm." Journal of Industrial Economics 20: 199-219.

Nelson, Richard R. and Sidney G. Winter (1982) An Evolutionary Theory of Economic Change. Cambridge, MA: Harvard University Press.

New York Times (1979) "How Springs Mills has been liquidating its losers." July 14: C30.

New York Times (1984a) "Employee ownership dream turns bitter for workers at Iowa meat plant." June 17: A-16.

New York Times (1984b) "Bank and U.S. Steel targets of Pittsburgh protest." July 23: A6.

New York Times (1984c) "Sheriff rebuffed in move to arrest cleric." November 10: A6.

New York Times (1984d) "Jailed minister vows to press jobless fight." December 11: B13.

New York Times (1985) "Worker-owned Rath Packing may be at the end of a long road." February 15: A16.

New York Times (1986a) "The steelworkers: limping at 50." June 15: D1, D29.

New York Times (1986b) "Early signs of promise in union 'partnership' at steel company." April 7: A8.

New York Times (1986c) "In withering city, steel dream turns desolate." February 5: A-16.

New York Times (1986d) "New steel company puts hope in castoffs." May 26: D5.

New York Times (1987a) "Hearst's eight-year buying spree." April 26: D-3.

New York Times (1987b) "USX: new optimism on steel." May 4: D1, D6.

Niskanen, William A., Jr. (1971) Bureaucracy and Representative Government. Chicago: Aldine.

Niskanen, William A., Jr. (1975) "Bureaucrats and politicians." Journal of Law and Economics 18: 617-643.

Osborn, Richard C. (1951) "Efficiency and profitability in relation to size." Harvard Business Review 20: 82-94.

Ouchi, William G. (1981) Theory Z. New York: Addison-Wesley.

Palmer, John (1973a) "The profit-performance effects of the separation of ownership from control in large U.S. industrial corporations." The Bell Journal of Economics and Management Science 4: 293-303.

Palmer, John (1973b) "The profit variability effects of the managerial enterprise." Western Economic Journal 11: 228-231.

Pascale, Richard Tanner and Anthony G. Athos (1981) The Art of Japanese Management. New York: Simon & Schuster.

Peters, Thomas J. and Robert H. Waterman, Jr. (1982) In Search of Excellence: Lessons from America's Best-Run Companies. New York: Harper & Row.

Pennings, Johannes W. (1982) "Organizational birth frequencies: an empirical investigation." Administrative Science Quarterly 27: 120-144.

Penrose, Edith Tilton (1952) "Biological analogies in the theory of the firm." American Economic Review 42: 804-819.

Pfeffer, Jeffrey (1972a) "Merger as a response to organizational interdependence." Administrative Science Quarterly 17: 382-394.

Pfeffer, Jeffrey (1972b) "Size and composition of corporate boards of directors." Administrative Science Quarterly 17.

Pfeffer, Jeffrey (1982) Organizations and Organization Theory. Marshfield, MA: Pitman.

Pfeffer, Jeffrey (1983) "Organizational demography," pp. 299-357 in L. L. Cummings and Barry M. Staw (eds.) Research in Organizational Behavior, Vol. 5. Greenwich, CT: JAI.

Pfeffer, Jeffrey and James Baron (1986) "Taking workers back out: recent trends in the structuring of employment." Research Paper No. 926, Graduate School of Business, Stanford University.

Pfeffer, Jeffrey and Alison Davis-Blake (1987) "The effect of the proportion of women on salaries." Administrative Science Quarterly 32: 1-24.

Pfeffer, Jeffrey and Huseyin Leblebici (1973) "Executive recruitment and the development of interfirm organizations." Administrative Science Quarterly 18: 449-461.

Pfeffer, Jeffrey and Phillip Nowack (1976) "Joint ventures and interorganizational interdependence." Administrative Science Quarterly 21: 398-418.

Pfeffer, Jeffrey and Gerald Salancik (1978) The External Control of Organizations: A Resource Dependence Perspective. New York: Harper & Row.

Pine, C. and S. Mundale (1983) "Til death do us part." Corporate Reports 14: 77-83.

Porter, Michael E. (1976) "Please note location of nearest exit: exit barriers and planning." California Management Review 19: 21-33.

Radice, H. K. (1971) "Control type, profitability, and growth in large firms." Economic Journal 81: 547-562.

Revans, R. W. (1958) "Human relations, management, and size," pp. 177-220 in F. M. Hugh-Jones (ed.) Human Relations and Modern Management. Amsterdam: North Holland.

Roethlisberger, F. J. and William J. Dickson (1939) Management and the Worker. Cambridge, MA: Harvard University Press.

Rosenblatt, P. C., L. De Mik, R. M. Anderson, and P. A. Johnson (1985) The Family in Business. San Francisco: Jossey-Bass.

Russell, Raymond (1984) Sharing Ownership in the Workplace. Albany, NY: State University of New York Press.

Savas, E. E. (1982) Privatizing the Public Sector. Chatham, NJ: Chatham House.

Scott, W. Richard (1975) "Organizational structure." Annual Review of Sociology 1: 1-20.

Scott, W. Richard (1987) Organizations: Rational, Natural, and Open Systems (2nd ed.). Englewood Cliffs, NJ: Prentice-Hall.

Selznick, Philip (1949) TVA and the Grass Roots. Berkeley: University of California Press.

Shirom, A. (1972) "The industrial relations systems of industrial cooperatives in the United States, 1880-1935." Labor History 13: 533-551.

Sills, David L. (1957) The Volunteers. New York: Free Press.

Simon, Herbert A. (1947) Administrative Behavior. New York: Macmillan.

Singh, Jitendra V., Robert J. House, and David J. Tucker (1986a) "Organizational legitimacy and the liability of newness." Administrative Science Quarterly 31: 171-193.

Singh, Jitendra V., Robert J. House, and David J. Tucker (1986b) "Organizational change and organizational mortality." Administrative Science Quarterly 31: 587-611.

Skocpol, Theda (1979) States and Social Revolutions: A Comparative Analysis of France, Russia, and China. New York: Cambridge University Press.

Starbuck, William (1965) "Organizational growth and development," pp. 451-533 in James G. March (ed.) Handbook of Organizations. Chicago: Rand McNally.

Starr, Paul (1982) The Social Transformation of American Medicine. New York: Basic Books.

Starr, Paul (1985) The Meaning of Privatization. Washington, DC: Economic Policy Institute.

Staw, Barry M. (1976) "Knee deep in Big Muddy: a study of escalating commitment to a chosen course of action." Organizational Behavior and Human Relations 16: 27-44.

Steer, Peter and John Cable (1978) "Internal organization and profit: an empirical analysis of large U. K. companies." Journal of Industrial Economics 27: 13-30.

Steckler, H. O. (1963) Profitability and Size of Firm. Berkeley: Institute of Business and Economic Research, University of California.

Stern, Robert N. and Tova H. Hammer (1978) "Buying your job: factors affecting the success or failure of employee acquisition attempts." Human Relations 31: 1101-1111.

Stern, Robert N., K. Hayden Wood, and Tova H. Hammer (1979) Employee Ownership and Plant Shutdowns. Kalamazoo, MI: Upjohn Institute.

Stewman, Shelby and Suresh L. Konda (1983) "Careers and organizational labor markets." American Journal of Sociology 88: 637-685.

Stigler, George J. (1947) Trends in Output and Employment. New York: National Bureau of Economic Research.

Stinchcombe, Arthur L. (1965) "Social structure and organizations," pp. 142-193 in James G. March (ed.) Handbook of Organizations. Chicago: Rand McNally.

Stinchcombe, Arthur L. (1983) Economic Sociology. New York: Academic Press.

Stinchcombe, Arthur L. (1986) "On social factors in administrative organization," pp. 221-230 in Arthur L. Stinchcombe (ed.) Stratification and Organization. Cambridge: Cambridge University Press.

Stodgill, Ralph (1974) Handbook on Leadership: A Survey of Theory and Research. New York: Free Press.

Tarrow, Sidney (1983) Struggling to Reform: Social Movements and Policy Change during Cycles of Protest. Ithaca, NY: Center for International Studies, Cornell University.

Teece, David J. (1987) "Applying concepts of economic analysis to strategic management," pp. 35-63 in David J. Teece (ed.) The Competitive Challenge: Strategies for Industrial Innovation and Renewal. Cambridge, MA: Ballinger Press.

Teece, David J. (1981) "Internal organization and economic performance: an empirical analysis of principal firms." Journal of Industrial Economics 30: 173-199.

Thibaut, J. W. and H. H. Kelly (1959) The Social Psychology of Groups. New York: John Wiley.

Thompson, James D. (1967) Organizations in Action. New York: McGraw-Hill.

Thompson, R. S. (1981) "Internal organization and profit: a note." Journal of Industrial Economics 30: 201-211.

Tilly, Charles (1978) From Mobilization to Revolution. Reading, MA: Addison-Wesley.

Tolbert, Pamela S. and Lynne G. Zucker (1983) "Institutionalized sources of change in the formal structure of organizations." Administrative Science Quarterly 28: 22-39.

Useem, Michael (1980) "Corporations and the corporate elite." Annual Review of Sociology 6: 41-77.

Vernon, J. (1972) Market Structure and Industrial Performance: A Review of Statistical Findings. Boston: Allyn and Bacon.

Von Mises, Ludwig (1944) Bureaucracy. New Haven, CT: Yale University Press.

Weber, Max (1946) "Bureaucracy," pp. 196-244 in H. H. Gerth and C. W. Mills (eds.) From Max Weber: Essays in Sociology. New York: Oxford University Press.

Weiss, Leonard W. (1971) "Quantitative studies of industrial organization," in M. Intrilligator (ed.) Frontiers of Quantitative Economics. Amsterdam: North Holland.

White, Harrison C. (1970) Chains of Opportunity: System Models of Mobility in Organizations. Cambridge, MA: Harvard University Press.

Williamson, Oliver E. (1975) Markets and Hierarchies. New York: Free Press.

Williamson, Oliver E. (1981) "The economics of organization: the transaction cost approach." American Journal of Sociology 87: 548-577.

Williamson, Oliver E. (1985) The Economic Institutions of Capitalism. New York: Free Press.

Williamson, Oliver E. (1987) "Transaction cost economics and organization theory." Paper presented to ISA-RC17 Workshop, Wassenaar, Netherlands.

Williamson, Oliver E. and Narottam Bhargava (1972) "Assessing and classifying the internal structure and control apparatus of the modern corporation," pp. 125-149 in Keith Cowling (ed.) Market Structure and Corporate Behaviour. London: Gray-Mills.

Winter, Sidney (1986) "Comments on Arrow and Lucas." Journal of Business 59: 385-399.

Woodward, Joan (1965) Industrial Organization: Theory and Practice. London: Oxford University Press.

Yuchtman, Ephraim and Stanley E. Seashore (1967) "A system resource approach to organizational effectiveness." American Sociological Review 32: 891-903.

Zald, Mayer (1978) "On the social control of industries." Social Forces 57: 66-71.

Zucker, Lynne G. (1987a) "Institutional theories of organization." Annual Review of Sociology 13: 443-464.

Zucker, Lynne G. (1987b) "Striking a balance: strike activity, unionization, and the employers' role, 1881 to 1887." Presented at the Institutional Theory Conference, Center for Advanced Study in the Behavioral Sciences, Stanford University, May 14-15.

Zucker, Lynne G. (1987c) "Normal change or risky business: institutional effects on the 'hazard' of change in hospital organizations, 1959-1979." Journal of Management Studies 24: 671-700.

Author Index

Subject Index

About the Authors

MARSHALL W. MEYER is Professor of Management and Anheuser-Busch Term Professor in the Wharton School and Professor of Sociology at the University of Pennsylvania. He has taught at Harvard, Cornell, and the University of California, Riverside, and has been a visiting professor at UCLA and the Yale School of Organization and Management. Some of his books include *Environments and Organizations* (with several coauthors), *Change in Public Bureaucracies, Limits to Bureaucratic Growth* and *Bureaucracy in Modern Society* (with Peter M. Blau). He is president of Research Committee 17, Sociology of Organizations, of the International Sociological Association. He has served on the editorial boards of the *American Sociological Review, Contemporary Sociology, Administrative Science Quarterly, Social Forces,* and *Social Science Quarterly,* and is currently associate editor of *Administrative Science Quarterly.*

LYNNE G. ZUCKER is an Associate Professor of Sociology; Affiliated Faculty Member, School of Education; Program Director for Organizational Research, Institute for Social Science Research; and Research Associate, Institute of Industrial Relations, all at UCLA. Recent visiting appointments include Yale and Harvard Business School. In 1987 she published "Insititutional Theories of Organization" in the *Annual Review of Sociology* and "Normal Change or Risky Business: Institutional Effects on the 'Hazard' of Change in Hospital Organizations, 1959-1979" in the *Journal of Management Studies.* She edited *Institutional Patterns and Organizations: Culture and Environment,* January 1988, which included her own chapter on institutional change processes. She has recently served on the ESRC/NSF Joint Committee on Comparative Binational Data, Council of the American Sociological Association's Organizations and Occupations Section, and on editorial boards of *American Journal of Sociology, American Sociological Review,* and *Administrative Science Quarterly.*